B/L 95   7.99

KU-826-610

BULLYING

WITHDRAWN

A Resource Guide
for
Parents and Teachers

Vivette O'Donnell
and the
Campaign against Bullying

NEWMAN COLLEGE
BARTLEY GREEN
BIRMINGHAM, 32

CLASS   371·58
BARCODE N0079054 0
AUTHOR   ODO

ATTIC PRESS
Dublin

Copyright © Vivette O'Donnell 1995

All rights reserved. Except for brief passages quoted in newspaper, magazine, television and radio reviews, no part of this book may be reproduced in any form or by any means, electronic or mechanical, including photocopying or recording, or by any information storage and retrieval systems without prior permission from the Publishers. This book is sold subject to the condition that it shall not, by way of sale or otherwise, be lent, resold, hired out or otherwise circulated in any form of binding or jacket other than that in which it is sold, and without a similar condition including this condition being imposed on the subsequent purchaser.

First published in Ireland in 1995 by
Attic Press
29 Upper Mount Street
Dublin 2

A catalogue record for this book is available from the British Library.

ISBN 1 85594 175 9

The moral right of the Author has been asserted.

Cover illustrations: Sheila Kern
Origination: Jimmy Lundberg Desktop Publishing
Printing: The Guernsey Press Co. Ltd

Attic Press receives financial assistance from the Arts Council/An Comhairle Ealaíon, Ireland.

To the memory of Cleo Nordi,
wonderful dancer and best of teachers.

CONTENTS

PREFACE

'BULLIED girl found hanged in bedroom.' 'What hope did I have when ten of them were beating the life out of me?' 'I'd rather die than go back to school.'

SUCH are the headlines that have appeared in our daily newspapers depicting the horrors of bullying. There is evidence from both empirical and anecdotal reports of the devastating effects which episodes of bullying can have on the lives of victims. The humiliation, fear, loneliness , frustration and loss of self-esteem which victims so often experience can lead in childhood to absenteeism from school and an inability to continue with education, and can be a source of depression, nervous breakdown and suicide. The effects among adult victims of bullying are very similar in that it is detrimental to their health, confidence, morale and performance. Children and adolescents who bully are also at risk. There is evidence to suggest that children who bully at school may go on to display more serious criminal behaviour and subject their families to domestic violence.

Vivette O'Donnell has been in the forefront in raising awareness about bullying in Ireland. She founded the Campaign against Bullying in 1983. The wealth of experience and depth of understanding that she has achieved through listening to victims of all ages is striking. It is her insights into bullying, its insidious and malicious nature, and her views on how those involved may be rehabilitated which makes this book so valuable and unique. Her rich source of information, written in a rather humorous and racy style, will complement and enlighten that which has been learned from empirical studies.

It is only in the last eight years that there has been any systematic study of bullying in Ireland. The studies have highlighted how prevalent the problem is. As many as one in ten schoolchildren at primary level are exposed to frequent bullying, and one in three to occasional bullying (O'Moore and Hillery, 1989). At post-primary level, preliminary results from the recent nationwide survey which I have conducted are indicating that 92,811 out of 348,927 pupils (27 per cent) are involved in bully/victim problems.

Vivette's book will be able to put a human face on these statistics. The suffering which she details is, therefore, by no means rare. On the contrary, there are too many children and adolescents in Ireland who are at risk of not realising their true potential. Initiatives must therefore be taken. The Department of Education has already made a significant contribution to preventing and dealing with bullying. National Guidelines on Countering Bullying Behaviour in Primary and Post-Primary Schools have been published. The teacher unions are also presently committed to creating in-service courses for their teachers. Furthermore, the Sticks and Stones Theatre Company helps to raise awareness of bullying in schools through the medium of drama. But once again, Vivette, in her book, is able to draw from her experiences in suggesting ways forward so that both school and workplace may become more harmonious. From reading her book, one can't help feeling that every effort should be made at pre-school and junior level to identify and remedy the behavioural patterns and environmental conditions that put children at risk of behaving as bullies. Thus we would go a long way in preventing the 'classroom bully', the 'teenage delinquent' and the 'violent adult'. This understandably requires resources. However, if education were to be perceived more as an investment rather than as an expense, society would undoubtedly benefit.

Mona O'Moore, PhD
Department of Teacher Education
Trinity College, Dublin.

FOREWORD

BULLYING is a notion which we associate with the school-yard, and the cruelty of boys to each other, with the stronger dominating the weak and so on.

But bullying can be a much more subtle activity than mere crude physicality. There are psychological bullies, moral bullies and social bullies. They exist all around us, and they are not confined to the schoolyard – or to boys!

We find them in every walk of life and at every age – people who attempt to dominate others unfairly, who insist that their point of view is the only one and who are intolerant and jealous of the success of others: people who, in short, have little respect for others.

I teach Speech and Drama professionally at primary, secondary and third level, and one of the constant problems I face is that of protecting the shy, the timid and the unsure from the type of pressure which bullies – the people who basically do not have the courage to perform themselves – apply. Ridicule is often their weapon, and it can have a devastating and lasting effect on a young person. And as an adjudicator of drama festivals around the country, I have occasionally been at the receiving end of this drama myself!

Vivette O'Donnell, whom I have known for many years, has been in the vanguard of the battle against bullying, and her dogged determination in continually bringing this problem to the attention of the public is deserving of support.

This is a timely book, and one which should be part of any home library. It is essential reading for all those involved with the education and guidance of young people.

Kate Canning, RSAMAD

Kate Canning graduated as a Speech and Drama teacher after a three-year combined course of studies at the Royal Scottish Academy of Music and Drama and the University of Glasgow. She holds a teaching diploma from Jordanhill College of Education. She has been a member both of British and Irish Actors Equity, and has taught at Carysfort College of Education and the Mater Dei Institute. She is a founder member of the Irish Association of Drama Adjudicators and currently teaches Speech and Drama at Blackrock College.

ACKNOWLEDGEMENTS

I AM VERY grateful to Ms Kate Canning and Dr Mona O'Moore for their gracious forewords.

Special thanks are due to Kate and Peter Canning, for without their encouragement and support in the early days of CaB, in the winter of 1983-84, the campaign might have faltered to a stop.

Dr Mona O'Moore's work on bullying is highly regarded both here and abroad. I would like to express my appreciation for her generosity and cooperation, especially with regard to the CaB conference on bullying in Trinity College, Dublin, in March 1993, and in connection with the development of the Sticks and Stones theatre company's school programmes.

I would like to thank all those who have contributed in any way to the CaB's efforts over the years, especially those like Rosemary and Catherine, Betty, Bobby, Gertie, Anne and Tony, Breda, Bernadette and others, who have worked on establishing local anti-bullying groups; also all the journalists who have helped the CaB, especially Phyllis Mitchell, editor of *Education Matters*. It has greatly encouraged me and the CaB to have contact with those engaged in countering bullying outside Ireland – a special thank you to those who have made personal contact.

Elizabeth Quinn, as coordinator of NAPS, National Association for Parents' Support, has also made an enormous difference to the scale and scope of anti-bullying work here, and is always a pleasure to work alongside.

Finally, and most of all, thank you to my dear friends and family, in particular my mother, my sister, Sylvia, and Brian, Hugh and Zoe.

Oh, of course – thank you to Ríona and Attic Press.

INTRODUCTION

BULLYING is a fact of life, and it is generally agreed that children will get into a lot of trouble if left to discover the facts of life for themselves.

Sooner or later you, as a parent, teacher, manager or victim, will need to know what to do about a bullying situation. This need to know is a very basic need. Many a person has told me, 'I didn't know what to do for the best. I didn't know which way to turn. I was afraid of making matters worse.' Most of these people were competent, capable people who knew the right thing to do in any situation until amazed and perplexed by the intransigence and complexity of a bullying problem. Bullying being the pervasive fact of life that it is, this means, of course, that they had already coped with some instances of bullying successfully or at least to their own satisfaction.

For bullying is very common. In that respect it is rather like arthritis. It is also like arthritis in that it comes in many different forms, all of them more or less painful and inconvenient. While some can be cleared up quickly and easily, others require long-term lifestyle management involving many complementary methods, treatments and strategies. The risks and ill-effects of ignorance and misinformation are equally similar. For example, if your arthritis involves inflammation, then movement, exercise, stress and strain will cause extra, avoidable damage, whereas if it is of the 'frozen shoulder' type, it is essential to ease some movement into it. In both cases it is disastrous to ignore the pain and carry on regardless.

Compare the pain of arthritis to the pain of being the target of verbal darts like 'Would you look at Bugs Bunny Teeth – what a twit.'

There are several ways to deal with this situation. If the speakers are total strangers it is best to 'ignore and avoid', because confrontation is unnecessary and could make matters worse. However, if the speakers are family, neighbours, fellow-pupils or colleagues, it is best to react at once to stop the discourtesy by replacing it with a pleasant or at least tolerable relationship. You could do any of the following:

- Say, 'I'd rather have Bugs Bunny teeth than halitosis.' This could be called the 'tit-for-tat method' – it shows that you can give as good as you get, and that nobody is going to get away with insulting you.
- You could say something nasty, cutting and offensive to the next person you meet that you dare to be rude to. That would be the 'pass it on' or 'do as you have been done to' method.
- You could say, 'I know you're only being nasty to me because you are hurting inside' – which is popularly known as psychobabble.
- You might say, 'I'm telling on you' and not follow through on your threat, thus achieving the worst of both worlds by giving the bully the ammunition of calling you 'rat' while not getting any back-up from authority for yourself.
- You could say nothing and go and tell, asking the person in charge to arrange supervision so that the jeerers can be caught in the act, reprimanded and reminded of the relevant social rule.
- You could face up to the speakers, making it clear that you take exception to what they said. If they are friendly in return that's good; and if they are not actually unpleasant that is satisfactory. But if they are unpleasant, you must then decide whether to warn them that you will tell if they persist, or just to go and tell, as you have already established that it was not a case of light-hearted teasing.

Whatever you do say to a bully must be your choice. Most people use phrases their parents or brothers and sisters use. If these don't work too well, listen and learn from those you mix with or from books, radio and TV. Bear in mind that you want relationships to keep getting better, not worse. You could try: 'Hey', 'Oy', 'I heard that', 'What did you just say?', 'What did you say that for?', 'What's the matter?', 'Did my ears deceive me or did you just say ...?'. If the reply is acceptable – for example 'Sorry', 'Only joking', 'No offence intended' – fine, and pausing for a chat can be a good idea. But if the reply is not acceptable, you need to decide how far you are going to pursue the attempt to sort things out face to face.

Anyone, whether or not they are the target of bullies, needs to get across the four-part message:

- I respect myself;
- I respect others;
- I expect others to respect me and each other;
- I will not tolerate disrespect.

This message is immeasurably important. Bear in mind, however, that those who assume that everything said to them is an offensive, insulting verbal attack are not displaying a confident expectation of respect: defensiveness and over-the-top reactions indicate a low level of confidence in oneself and/or in others – a loss of trust which is an obstacle to building good relationships and establishing a good atmosphere.

This partly explains the appeal of tit-for-tat. Tit-for-tat also suggests a feeling of equality – but unfortunately the equality involved is that of being equally insulted, equally hurt, equally deprived, equally dead. The 'feel-good factor' of tit-for-tat is made up partly of 'I got my own back', and partly of 'I stopped a nuisance'. The former is revenge, which may be sweet but which is also unwholesome. The latter is good but very infrequent; where tit-for-tat works to stop a nuisance, the words 'Don't' or 'Stop it' or 'Never do that again' would work even better.

Unfortunately, like arthritis, sometimes bullying has no cure. However, even in these cases it is possible to alleviate pain. And remember, there are many forms of both bullying and arthritis which can been fully and completely cured. Even where the situation is very difficult, at least some improvements can be made.

This is a self-help guide for those who want to prevent bullying from occurring where they live and work, and for those who, being aware of a problem caused or exacerbated by bullying, want to deal with it successfully by eradicating all forms of abuse and cruelty completely, or at least by greatly reducing the incidence and severity and the ignorance and passive tolerance of bullying. Combating bullying is obviously difficult and therefore daunting. However, it is not impossible, for it has been done, and it makes sense to use methods and tools which have worked well for other people.

I hope this book will help you with your bullying problem. I suggest that you read it straight through once to discover what it contains, and to get an overall picture of what bullying is and of what is involved in tackling it. Then the book can be used as a resource guide whenever the need arises: for example, you may wish to look up W for Workplace Bullying or S for Stress. There are lists of causes, effects and signs of bullying, and suggestions for rehabilitation, mediation, games and strategies. Everything included has been proved useful in real cases known to me as a result of eleven years' experience with CaB.

It only remains for me to wish you well. Now read on.

Vivette.
January 1995

Achievers

FOR MANY reasons, achieving is an important issue for anyone concerned about bullying. There is a common belief that all bullies are low achievers. Some are, of course, but others are top of their class, admired and successful.

Nobody is ever purely a high or low achiever; everyone, after all, is a non-achiever at what they've never attempted. Clearly, however, to achieve at something you need enough confidence to make an attempt. You also need motivation, whether it comes from genuine interest or incentives such as rewards, prizes, a desire to please, flattery, competitive instinct, coercion or necessity.

We know from common sense, personal experience, and experiments on rats and other animals that successes encourage us to strive longer and harder. One experiment on rats placed in a tank of water established quite predictably that those which were lifted out of the tank before they stopped swimming would swim for longer next time, whereas those that were not rescued till they sank from exhaustion would sink sooner next time. Success builds on success and failure promotes giving up. Similarly, cats soon lose interest in chasing a string or ribbon they never catch, or one which they catch too easily. Striving requires both success and purpose such as demonstration of skill or progress or money.

Because we all enjoy being good at something, we are inclined to spend both more time and more effort on what we are good at. Therefore the achievement gap widens. Expectations of success or confidence, based on experience of achieving, greatly enhance concentration power and chances of success.

Self-willed, self-indulgent children may resist adult authority every step of the way; they accept that adults have the right to make them do things, but they will do nothing unless they are made to. Some are quite sweet and polite about it; some are a bit sulky and some are rude and swear and shout and even hit out at people before storming off.

As long as studying, doing school lessons and practising the piano or whatever are regarded by a child as 'work and duty done for other people only because they want it', that child is likely to underachieve.

In summary: to achieve you need *confidence* and *motivation*. Motivation comes from two carrots – interest and incentives – and two sticks – coercion and the necessity for survival. Confidence and success build on each other.

What helps a child to achieve is a combination of motivations:

- the goal must be made attractive so that the child will want to achieve at it;
- the child should be helped to enjoy the feeling that comes with success;
- the child should have the final motivation of rewards and reinforcers such as praise and little gold stars;
- the child should be encouraged to develop a strong sense of duty and pride so that he will not want to let either himself or his family, neighbourhood, club or school down.

It is important that the child realises that some of what achieving a desired goal entails will not be enjoyable at all. Children will usually ask about these things, but unfortunately the quite sensible question 'Is that really necessary? Why?' is usually expressed as 'Do I have to?' – something that can irritate colleagues, parents and teachers who may snap, 'Yes, because I say so. Just do it.' Sometimes, indeed, the task or procedure is not necessary or there is a better way; if that seems to be the case everyone should be encouraged to ask, 'Please explain why this is so important' or 'Could this be done in another way?'

So what does this have to do with bullying?

Achievement can affect the form which bullying can take, and the effects of bullying can be associated with levels of achievement.

High Achievers

High achievers may *bully* each other from jealousy and as part of competition. Their teachers and parents may condone this bullying behaviour, seeing it as an example of the dominant leadership qualities necessary to get on in the world. Where teachers and parents disapprove of bullying, the high-achieving bullies are clever enough to hide most of their bullying, and to explain away or find justification for any that is spotted.

High achievers may be *victims* of the above bullying from peers who pour scorn on slips, mistakes, apparent failures or shortcomings. They'll also be targeted by low achievers who will suggest that they are weird, unpopular, goody-goodies, licks, swots or snobs, and that they are missing out on a 'normal' life – a jibe that is especially effective as childhood and youth are fleeting and unrepeatable. Regrets at missing something supposedly essential to a proper, real, full or natural young existence can last a lifetime.

As education aims to develop students' critical faculty, and as students receive a great deal of more or less helpful and constructive criticism, they can themselves become overly critical, impatient and judgemental without feeling in the least responsible for any resultant injuries. In this they can be like someone who drives too fast, without a thought for the safety or wellbeing of others, simply for the pleasure of speed and power.

Middling Achievers

Even high-achieving perfectionists are middling achievers in many areas, if only for lack of time – housekeeping, parenting, cooking, sewing, engineering or languages are examples of such areas. Middling achievers at school can *bully* high achievers to come down to their level so that the teacher doesn't expect such high standards from the whole class. They often bully both each other and low achievers for slips, mistakes and for not conforming. Middling achievers prize solidarity more than individuality.

Middling achievers are *victims* in various ways and for a

variety of reasons. Firstly, they may be under pressure to do better than they are able – they have the intelligence but not the stamina to do well in every subject. Middling achievers in a small class like Honours Physics may do badly, as they can be reluctant to ask questions because the Grade A students sigh about 'waste of class time' and 'hasn't got the brains for this, shouldn't be here'. Grade As often take it amiss when an erstwhile Grade C or D excels in some test or exercise or simply moves up to Grade B or A, while the Grade Ds may interpret the move as rejection and retaliate by bullying.

A similar situation may occur when a student wins a prize, for although they are fine rewards to be used as motivation, prizes can backfire. If you are jubilant at winning a prize it is easier for others to accept that you worked for it and appreciate it; and you will hardly notice their jealousy if you are so pleased with the prize. But if, for example, it is announced that there will be a prize for the student with the best Science exam marks in third year, and the winner feels that's nice but no big deal, the wave of jealousy, disappointment and resentment can be shocking. Sometimes, too, there is fine irony, where a bully-gang wins a prize for an anti-bullying project such as a poster competition.

Low Achievers
There are two types of low achievers: firstly those who perform poorly through no fault of their own but because of disadvantage, illness, handicap or disability, or undiagnosed specific learning difficulty. Secondly, there are those who have the potential to do well but underachieve because they don't pay attention, don't concentrate, don't exert themselves, don't work hard or study either in class or at home.

Where does bullying come into all this? The answer, as usual, is complex, but centres on the child's perceptions of what is his due and on his feelings of being deprived, hurt, humiliated, resentful, jealous and angry. Such feelings can give rise both to bullying behaviour and victim behaviour, corresponding to some extent to 'acting-out' and 'acting-in'.

Teachers complain of disruptive pupils who are 'unmotivated underachievers'. If you talk and listen to schoolchildren you find that several beliefs contribute to continued underachieving:

'I know I can't do this because I lack natural ability.'

'I know I can't do this because I never bothered to learn the basics in primary school.'

'I fell behind when I was sick.'

'Getting the right answers depends on inspired guess-work' – this is most likely in teenagers who have seldom worked a problem out logically from first principles, and is common in maths exams.

'I could do it if I were interested and really worked at it, but it is not interesting and doing it won't solve my problems or cheer me up.'

'Maybe even if I studied hard I would still do badly and that would mean I'm stupid as well as lazy and rebellious. I'd rather not know.'

'Bright kids don't study.'

'My friends won't like me if I swot.'

'I did work for that exam and I still got an F – never mind I just did four or five hours' chaotic hard slog the night before and the achievers did three hours a week for the past thirty school weeks.'

As always, to sort it out it is necessary to talk it out. The underachiever's beliefs must be expressed and discussed.

Acronyms

THIS CHAPTER evolved when I was playing with ideas for a *New Scientist* backronym competition in 1994 while also trying to develop ways of using Linda Frost's observation that children at school can be divided into several categories. These are as follows:

- those who sometimes bully others, called 'bullies' for short but never labelled as such;
- those who sometimes are bullied, called 'victims' for short but equally never labelled as such;
- those who sometimes bully and sometimes are bullied, called 'bully-victims' for short but not labelled as such;
- those who keep aloof, called 'outsiders'; and
- 'sages', who are never bullies and never bullied.

The ideal, is obviously, for us all to be Sages. This involves determining the qualities and personalities of Sages, what they say and do, and then adapting our own behaviour and developing desirable characteristics.

We are all born with the potential to be loving, practical, compassionate and fair, but our development tends to be haphazard and chance also plays a large part in determining our role-models. Making a definite decision and conscious choice to change ourselves can result in huge improvements while increasing rather than diminishing our individuality. However, there is always resistance to change, especially of oneself.

A good way to get around resistance to change is through the use of games such as devising acronyms and backronyms. To show how games might be used in a school, to make us more like Sages, I wrote the following acronyms to describe some instantly recognisable types of pupil, teacher and parent. You could use this to get a discussion going. The class could make up their own acronyms – remember to say they do not have to be animals.

DOGS are Dutiful, Obedient, Good, Successful.
CATS are Clever, Able, Tricky, Successful.
RATS are Rogues, Aggressive, Troublesome, Sly.
MICE are Meek, Insignificant, Craven, Excluded.
SAGES are Sagacious, Admired, Graceful, Even-handed, Spirited.
LIONS are Loving, Intelligent, Open, Nice, Scholarly.
TIGERS are Teacherish, Impatient, Generous, Energetic, Resourceful, Superior.
BEARS are Boring, Exacting, Argumentative, Ridiculous, Stupid.
BULLS are Bad, Unfair, Lying, Lazy, Selfish.
SHEEP are Silly, Helpless, Envious, Eager, Puny.
GOATS are Great, Organised, Affable, True, Sure.

Sages admire Dogs and Cats, Lions, Tigers and Goats. They tend to be unaware that everyone else admires them.

The children might like to play act being the acronym animals described here as an activity in drama class. Obviously, these tags are not intended as lifelong labels – I believe that, although some people are blessed with a greater intelligence or more robust physical strength than others, everyone can choose which qualities to develop.

(See **Personality Types** *and* **Games**.*)*

Action

'The first time I was bullied at school I told my mother and she went up to the school and talked to the teacher. The teacher was very nice and promised that action would be taken, and the next day action was taken – the bullies were punished. But the bullies were very angry, and they beat me up and called me a tell-tale and a sissy. The other children called me a rat over and over again. This was much worse than the original bullying had been. So I decided never to tell again. I was bullied a lot but I never told again. Sometimes the teachers or the principal found out about the bullying and when they did they never condoned it. Action was always taken, but it only meant I got bullied even worse. My parents and teachers did their best but there was nothing they could do to stop the bullying. People in authority can apply the rules, but the bullies will always be able to get you for it. They did their best, and action was always taken, but the bullying only stopped the year I did the School Leaving (certificate exams) because at the school I went to nobody bullied the sixth years.'

THIS IS a sad tale. Sad because it is typical of so many. Sad because of the suffering. Saddest because of the depressing, defeatist message that bullying can't be stopped.

It is also a very frustrating tale. How were those in authority to know that the action taken had made matters worse? If only they had been told, further measures could have been taken until the problem really had been dealt with and the bullying had been stopped.

Sometimes the victims of bullying do tell someone in authority, and sometimes 'action is taken'. If it is, the victims often suffer even more as a consequence, and so they decide to keep any further bullying secret. But such victims hotly defend the authorities, saying, 'When bullying was reported they took action.' They appreciate the fact that the authorities did not blame the victim, as often happens, but

12

did their best and made the disapproval of the bullying clear. The victims regard the problem as intractable and point out that the authorities can hardly be blamed for failure, since nobody told them that their best had not been good enough.

That last point is certainly fair: surveillance cannot be one hundred per cent, and nor can foresight, nor training, nor any kind of system for communication, if folk choose not to communicate. Imagine if someone took the same attitude to a plumber: 'I told the plumber about the leaking pipe and action was taken; he came up and worked on it, but it was leaking again by the next day. I know the plumber did his best, but after months of living with that pipe leaking I could stand it no longer and was forced to move house.'

It is not true that the problem of bullying is usually intractable. Keeping the fact that you are being bullied a secret means that you will continue to be a victim indefinitely or until one of these happens: the bullies decide to stop bullying you; the bullies go away; you move away; or you acquire strength and skills which enable you to stop the bullies yourself. Sometimes you get the help you need by good luck or fate: this happens in *Anne of Windy Willows*, where Anne is now a graduate teacher. She is no longer bullied when the clan find out that she has discovered some information about an ancestor of theirs which they do not wish to become public knowledge. The bullies do not realise that Anne is too honourable to use the information to hurt them – a fact worth remembering when dealing with a long-term, dyed-in-the-wool bully. Indeed, if the victim can survive the bullying itself, there is every hope that it will end – when, for example, s/he leaves school or home. But it is much better for everyone if the victim, with the help of others, can stop the bullying as quickly as possible.

There is a great deal of material available now, in this book and in others, which can be used by those in authority to stop or control a bullying problem. It is well worth while for people who are victims or aware of bullying to report it to those in authority so that an effective course of action can be followed.

When considering a course of action it makes sense to ask:

- *'Who gets helped by this and will they also be hurt?'*
- *'Who gets hurt by this and will they also be helped?'*
- *'Can changes be made to this course of action so that the level of help increases and the amount of hurt is lessened?'*
- *'Is there a better course of action which we could take?'*

Inaction and making matters worse are not satisfactory choices. What is desired is not an event but a course of action – a *series* of events – that ends when a desired result, such as the former bully being rehabilitated, is achieved. In short, don't think in terms of *taking action* but rather of *following a course of action* to remedy bullying.

- *'What is the best course of action?'* This is a sensible question but a difficult one for anyone to answer, as it is hard to cover every eventuality.

First start with step one. Action to cure bullying is like action to restore good health: whether or not there is a helpful prescription, there will always be also a lot of lifestyle Do's and Don'ts to follow. Just as the person told to walk at least a mile a day usually comes to enjoy that daily walk, as well as benefiting from the exercise, so a lot of the discussions and conversations, games and role-play exercises used to counter bullying can bring some unexpected bonuses.

Authority

IF YOU, as a parent, teacher, employer, manager or law-enforcement officer, are in a position of authority, it is as well to be aware that it is in the interest of bullies to attack authority figures and rules, and to cause confusion: where an authority figure is at fault, a bully will home in, not on the fault or the figure, both of which deserve censure, but on the fact that authority exists at all.

Everybody has some power, and power tends to corrupt; therefore it is necessary to have rules and regulations, contracts, codes of behaviour, laws, house rules et cetera, all of which are based on principles drawn from the rights, needs and responsibilities of humans, and ultimately based on the idea of right versus wrong.

Bullies do not wait for people to abuse their power. For example, they will home in on any child who is feeling down because of a parental 'No', and will try to convince as many people as possible that that child is hard done by. If a confused, well-meaning 'bleeding heart' takes up this cause, enormous harm can be done. Even if the bullies succeed only in wasting time while parents and teachers clear up the confusion, even if only one child is influenced to behave badly, it is a victory to the bullies – they have won a fight against authority and demonstrated their power.

Those in authority need to come to terms with the fact that while some bullies are simple bullies, others have been coached in bullying by older experts such as their big brothers and sisters.

The ideal example of a simple bully is the boy of eight who pinches a girl's arm and never does it again once she pinches him back. Another example is the boy of ten who provokes another boy into beating him in a 'fair fight', after which they are friends for life; or the twelve-year-old girl who approaches a new pupil and demands his lunch money.

The boy refuses and threatens to tell the teacher; the bully retires defeated.

Too many people love the story of the cheeky bully who never gave bother after someone in authority gave him a 'good thrashing'.

Considering how easily simple bullies are dealt with, it is surprising, but regrettably common, to find adult bullies of this sort.

Simple bullies are successful because:

- the victim is unprepared;
- the victim is afraid (simple fear);
- the victim has come off worse in previous encounters with bullies (acquired fear).

However, everybody in authority needs to be aware of the fact that not all bullies are simple bullies.

For example, a more sophisticated bully-boy of eight would give pinches that would hurt a bit but whose mark would vanish after half a minute. As soon as the victim retaliates (ineffectively) by pinching him back, he yells, 'Ow, Teacher, she pinched me.' Teacher says, 'Did you pinch him? His arm is marked and yours is not.' Bully: 'I was only teasing, I didn't hurt her.' Teacher to victim: 'There was no need to pinch him so hard.'

This situation is depressingly common: often the victim's heavy punch to end the bullying is used to put the victim in the wrong with the authorities. This is a victory for the bully and for injustice. After many such incidents, children come to believe that life is not fair, teachers are unfair, companions don't help you when you are in the right, and authority and justice don't go together.

In conclusion: if you are in a position of authority and attempting to cope with a bullying problem, tell people not to hit out unless it is the only option open to them; whenever possible, they should get away from trouble and report it – as in the Stay Safe advice.

Do exercise your authority on behalf of justice. Very few

cases are too trivial to bother about. Intervene sooner rather than later.

Remember that the real work of stopping and preventing bullying is carried out by the people on the spot: by family members, neighbours, teachers, juvenile liaison and neighbourhood-watch officers, et cetera.

If someone has been marked out as a victim by a bully-gang, try to give that person protection by family, teachers, schoolfellows and gardaí/police. Also try to get the bully-gang to change their behaviour to what is acceptable – catch them out and caution them, following up as necessary.

Warn kids that bully-gangs recruit from those who break rules, so they should not break even trivial rules.

Remember that when those in charge fail to keep good order, people may take the law into their own hands. The result is, at best, very rough justice. Innocent people have been killed by lynch mobs; people guilty of relatively minor offences have had arms and legs broken by outraged citizens.

Nip trouble in the bud and it need never lead to serious injury, damage or court cases. It will, instead, lead to genuine and well-deserved liking and respect for you, as the person in authority, and for everyone else.

Sometimes!

Avoiding Bullying

THE FOLLOWING points are aimed mainly at school-goers who may be victims of bullying, but they should prove useful to anyone suffering from this problem.

DON'T BOAST, sneer, act the fool, shout (except for help in an emergency or for other good reason), be impatient, complain, whinge, whine, defend the indefensible, state weird or controversial views, attract unwanted attention, buy 'friendship', lend or borrow or give anything if you think people are trying to find out if you are soft, have anything odd with you, let anyone 'mess' with your things, let anyone push you around or call you names, get into fights or quarrels or demonstrations against authority, seem to have more money than sense.

Never say 'That's silly' or 'You are being silly'. Say 'I don't agree' or 'Stop messing'. Do obey school rules. Do have everything you bring to school marked with your name in both an obvious and a secret place so it can be identified if stolen. Do sit beside a wall and near the teacher's desk. Do have a quiet word with the teacher at the end of the lesson (unless she is in a hurry) if anyone is pestering/bullying you. Do report in a quiet, restrained manner any bullying outside the classroom – not just of yourself but of other pupils if you observe any – to the vice-principal, dean, guidance counsellor, matron, year-master or favourite teacher.

Work through the Department of Education *Guidelines on Countering Bullying*, the Stay Safe notes and this book with a friend and/or family.

Copy the cat. If you annoy a cat it glares at you; say 'Sorry, Puss,' and you're slowly forgiven. Copy the cat's technique: if a bully annoys you, glare and use suitable phrases, then cautiously accept an apology.

Decide your aims and goals. In general people want appreciation, which can be shown through money, thanks, applause and respect. People you respect think well of you. People you respect treat you with good manners, fair play and consideration – they are positive, not negative. You will often get the first without the second – too bad!

Remember that being used is not the mark of a victim. It proves you are useful and you get appreciation and respect for it. Being abused *is* the mark of a victim, especially when it is followed by ineffective retaliation – that is, behaviour that makes matters worse. Before speaking or doing anything in response to a bully, make sure it is not ineffective retaliation.

Keeping these aims in view, identify problems. Find solutions to problems.

Negotiate. Compromise is usually necessary. Timing is crucial, so if possible wait for the perfect moment: arrange a meeting to sort things out and stick to the agenda. Having made an agreement, do not grumble about the terms. Find solutions to any problems as a matter of course.

When deciding your priorities, remember: clarity avoids conflict. A performance/interview/exam takes precedence over a rehearsal. A rehearsal takes precedence over a lesson, and a lesson takes precedence over ordinary pastimes or recreations. Traditionally the system looks something like this: my god (morality/standards/ideals/sense of right and wrong) over myself over my family over my work (and/or studies) over my friends/hobbies, over my acquaintances.

Once you decide your own priorities, stick to them. Explain your priorities to friends and relations; righteous indignation of family is not a helpful thing. Don't let them upset your plans.

Find ways to let off steam that won't lessen people's regard for you.

Remember, people are people – not their collection of 'glittering prizes'. What matters is what they think, what they feel, how they behave.

Aim to be quietly popular with most people, especially

those generally respected. People are more likely to help people they like and respect.

How to Get On Well at School

Always be polite. Be formal to teachers, but use informal language to fellow pupils. Obey rules. Always be as well groomed as the average pupil in the top class. Don't stick out like a sore thumb. Do not cause a scene, but do not be a doormat; use words and phrases, like those suggested in this book, to deal with awkward situations.

At a new school, club or other group, do not make friends with the first person who approaches you to chum up. Good manners mean that you must not rebuff a friendly approach, but that's not the same as becoming bosom buddies straight away. Sensible people wait to find out what you are like before offering friendship. The people who would be worth having as good friends have some friends already and are sensible. Pay attention, watch and listen, and soon you will know who is good company and of good character; make friends with them.

Work hard at lessons. Cooperate and participate pleasantly in class. Develop and use a pleasant sense of humour. Observe Be Safe, Keep Safe rules – stay in sight of staff so you can't be assaulted. Join school clubs that appeal to you – the chess club, the debating society, whatever. These give you something to do, and companions with similar interests. Be nice to chat to – not sneering and not flattering.

Here are useful phrases. Think about when you would use them, what the riposte would be, what you would reply. Practise the ones that fit your style so you are well prepared for dealing effectively with attempts to bully you.

- 'What do you think you're doing?'
- 'Never ever do that again.'
- 'What do you mean?'
- 'What makes you say that?'
- 'Why?'
- 'Do you have a problem?'

- 'Is anything bothering you?'
- 'What do you want me to do?'
- 'No.'
- 'Not likely.'
- 'Forget it.'
- 'You must be joking.'
- 'Too much hassle.'
- 'Suppose I tell X what you just said?'
- 'No. My parents are very strict/No. My parents would freak.'
- 'No. My mother's not well, I don't want to worry her.'
- 'No. I've to be at home/school in five minutes or they'll come looking for me.'
- 'No. I promised I'd do something else.'
- 'Was that intentional?'
- 'I don't think that's any of your business.'
- 'I think you owe me an apology.'
- 'It's not telling tales – it's telling to be safe.'
- 'I have rights, you know.'
- 'You're mistaken.'
- 'Very funny. Ha, ha.' 'Really'/'Gosh'/'Wow.'
- 'I've heard about you.'
- 'Excuse me.'
- 'Thanks, I don't think.'
- 'Sure, any time.'
- 'Hey. Watch it. Steady on.'
- 'Don't do that.'
- 'Not a good idea.'
- 'Hold it, (teacher's name) is looking at us' (need not be true).
- 'Sorry. I'm busy.'/'Sorry. Must dash.'
- 'Did you do that on purpose?'
- 'Are you a bully?'
- 'I've got an awful temper but I've just about learnt to control it.'
- 'I know how you feel.' 'I do understand.' 'Believe me, I do sympathise.'
- 'Is that so?'

- 'What a shame.'
- 'Tough.'
- 'Cut it out'/'Cool it.'
- 'Do you want to talk about this?'
- 'I'm really sorry for you.'
- 'You're right.'
- 'Okay'/'sure.'
- 'Would you like a mediator?'

Remember the distinction between cowardice and caution, aggressiveness and assertiveness, bravado and courage.

Effective retaliation is a course of action, such as agreeing to mediation, which stops the bullying abuse without loss of grace or face on your side. You may also get reparation, for example an apology or payment of costs. When dealing with friends, relations and colleagues, keep pain, grief and loss of face to a minimum – hopefully they will do the same when you are at fault.

Really effective retaliation spots the trouble coming and prevents it. Anticipation allows you to nip trouble in the bud, the sooner the better. Be realistic – nobody can solve everybody's problems, and nobody can always solve their own problems in a way that fully pleases them. You can stop the abuse, but you may lose something else as well, so be clear about your priorities: it is better for a school to lose one disruptive pupil than to let the pupil go on behaving badly.

Other people do not share all your views and standards – sometimes you must agree to differ, or even, though not often, agree to part.

Remember that competition and cooperation are good and positive, while jealousy, envy, back-stabbing and rivalry are bad and negative. Not knowing your good points is stupid, not modest. Try for balance.

Live and let live. Don't be a victim. Don't be a bully.

Blame

'Who deserves the credit? Who deserves the blame?' Tom Lehrer

HOW NICE it would be to wipe out the words, the very concepts of blame, fault, and guilt. But it can't be done. We would still know in our hearts if something was our fault, if we were to blame. Also, we all want to have rights – and with rights come responsibilities, and responsibilities lead to credit and blame.

Nobody likes to be to be to blame, to be at fault, to feel shame, humiliation and guilt. Since any form of dishonesty virtually always makes matters worse, denial and shifting the blame where it does not belong are not recommended. Fairness, ready acceptance of apologies, making light of the matter, some not too onerous form of reparation or restitution, and an understanding that none of us is 100 per cent perfect can make the experience bearable and help everyone to cope next time.

Children need a lot of help coping with blame and shame. They need plenty of role-models so they can learn to say, 'Sorry, it was my fault, what can I do to put things right?' Clearly, parents and teachers are the principal role-models, and teachers who admit very openly the occasional mistakes they make earn children's respect, and help them to relax and concentrate instead of being tense and anxious about slipping up. More help is available from storybooks, plays, films et cetera. It is impossible to exaggerate the importance of this – every year youngsters run away from home or take their own lives because they are unable to cope with being to blame for something relatively trivial like crashing the family car.

If problems come to light as a result of some failure, then good can come of the event, provided that the problems are attended to. After a disaster or a near-disaster, it is important to apportion blame so that a course of action can be undertaken to lessen the likelihood of a similar disaster in the future. Too often, as with roll-on roll-off ferries, not enough heed is paid to problems and their causes; even where the cause of an accident is not man-made, such as when someone is struck by lightning, there will be lessons about safety skills and statistical likelihood to be learnt. The greater the human input, the more lessons to be learnt and the more measures, including legislation, to be taken.

To take a bullying example, say that a pupil at school pulls a knife on another pupil. It is not enough that the knife-wielder be suspended or expelled. A very full investigation needs to be carried out, involving all the pupils, teachers, parents and others who have relevant knowledge of the children involved. There may be need for post-traumatic counselling; there is greater need to find out all the ramifications behind what led up to the dramatic event. Then policies must be devised and followed so that in future help is given early and problems nipped in the bud. The main culprit is never the only person at fault.

Too often all that is done as the result of a problem coming to light is the apportioning of blame, which can result in people taking sides with increasing ill-feeling. Everyone needs to remember that the aim must be for all to be accountable and to take responsibility for their own actions, and for everyone to do whatever they can to help to put things right as far as that is possible.

LM Montgomery's *Anne* books and CS Lewis's *Narnia* books are particularly helpful as well as enjoyable.

*(See also **Responsibility** and **Rights**.)*

Bully-Victims

A BULLY-VICTIM is someone who is a victim of abuse some of the time, but who also displays various forms of aggressive bullying behaviour some of the time. The disruptive, badly behaved underachiever in primary school, the mitcher who drops out of secondary school, and the vast majority of convicted criminals are bully-victims rather than pure bullies.

Revenge is the bully-victim's principal motivation, though a lot of his bad behaviour is just habit. The bully-victim takes his bad temper out on everybody, but, faced with authority figures, his behaviour may take the form of sullenness or whinging, whereas he may be viciously cruel to someone weaker. Another way in which bully-victims 'get back at' authority figures is by vandalism: graffiti, joy-riding, breaking windows, arson. Their behaviour is rightly called 'looking for attention'; they feel sore, let down and undervalued, especially because they believe they are seen as unimportant. Sometimes such a bully-victim will get pleasure from a wrongdoing – 'Well, you noticed that!'

When told off for their bullying behaviour, bully-victims claim to be very hard done by – that is, they claim to be victims without actually using the word. Though they clearly feel like victims a lot of the time, only a few will admit to being bullied or 'picked on'; the rest focus on the other bullies' behaviour – 'He was being a pain. They were annoying me'. This latter type of bully-victim will deny vehemently that they were ever victims of bullying, but they will claim to be hard done by if they are in trouble for anything, especially for aggression. 'They started it. Nobody hits me and gets away with it. She called me names last week.' They try to make out that it was acceptable tit-for-tat, a fair fight or self-defence.

Occasionally bully-victims are, or feel, trapped in a gang of bad companions, up to their neck in trouble, afraid but unable to escape.

A bully-victim is the hardest of all to rehabilitate, and this is dealt with in detail in the chapter on **Rehabilitation.**

(See also **Acronyms, Lies/Deceit in Bullying** and **Workplace Bullying.**)

Bystanders

THE 1993 Sheffield Anti-Bullying Project describes four kinds of bystanders – those who:

- *actively encourage* the bad behaviour;
- *passively support* the bad behaviour;
- *passively reject* the bad behaviour;
- *actively challenge* the bad behaviour.

To eliminate bullying it is necessary for bystanders to belong only to the final two categories. It helps to have a school rule which states that 'There is no such thing as an innocent bystander; witnesses should stop abuse or get help to have it stopped'.

How can pupils be motivated actively to challenge bullying behaviour? The answer is by simple training, as with safety skills and first aid. If the problem is easy to handle, children should be taught to handle it themselves. For example, if someone calls a Nigerian boy a racist name, a bystander can say, 'Hey, watch it, you! That's racist talk.' Or, perhaps, a group of friends see younger children bullying. The older children should be encouraged to go over and say: 'What's the problem? What is this all about? Do you want us to help you sort it out or do we call a teacher?' And, a tip from the Sages: the question 'Is this really necessary, lads?' has been found very effective when used by sixth-year schoolgirl bystanders to stop their classmates when their pranks degenerate into bullying.

If you do see someone behaving badly, don't comment – command! Don't say, 'What a way to behave!', 'Did you ever see the like?' or 'Some people'. Say, 'Stop that', 'Don't do that', 'What do you think you're doing?', 'Move'. Don't be fazed by 'What authority do you have?', 'What right have you to interfere?' or other challenges of that sort. You have rights and authority by virtue of the community to which you belong.

In some cases the problem is not easy to handle, and bystanders will need help. Consider the following situation and your options. Suppose you see somebody being attacked (or assaulted) by someone who is armed with a knife or a gun. What should you do? Here are the most likely answers:

- 'Don't get involved – get away to safety'
- 'Go to help the person being attacked'
- 'Get help – call the police/gardaí from the nearest public telephone box'
- 'Tell someone and keep telling till someone believes you'
- 'Scream.'

You will get these replies from many decent, competent, intelligent achievers, as well as from those less capable and less successful. Let us look at these answers, one at a time.

Don't get involved – get away to safety

This is a most popular piece of advice, often given by parents to their children. Such parents also say, 'Fight your own corner,' because they recognise that if everyone refuses to get involved, there is never going to be any help coming your way. It is chilling to hear someone say, 'Don't get involved and get away to safety.' It does not cross their mind that you might summon help with no risk to yourself, benefiting the victim if help arrives in time, and benefiting the community if the assailant is apprehended. It does not even occur to this person that if the attacker is not caught, the next victim could be him/herself.

Perhaps you don't want to risk having to go to court as a witness. But you can report an incident without agreeing to appear as a witness. (If you are called as a witness, Victim Support will give you help and advice.)

People will also advise you never to go anywhere dangerous, but to stay 'where it is safe'. Unfortunately there is no such place. Nowhere is completely safe – all we can do is to teach children how to be as safe as possible.

Go to help the person being attacked
Given that the assailant has a knife or gun, it is scary to hear someone who does not have specialist combat skills say they would risk such serious injury to themselves while having so little chance of actually helping the original victim. However foolhardy, the person who says this does have great and admirable courage, and it is the fact that their action is very unlikely to help the victim that convinces them not to rush into personal danger.

Get help – call the police/gardaí
Most attacks happen in heavily populated areas, such as cities, towns and their suburbs, and that means the nearest telephone is rarely more than 100 yards away. Even in a remote area, getting to a phone is usually an essential part of a rescue. Lots of people believe they can use only their own phone or a public phone box. In an emergency you can ask anyone who has a phone to telephone the police/gardaí and the ambulance/fire brigade services for help. You may be regarded with suspicion, especially by a householder. Agree to their phoning for help; you should not insist on entering their premises. If you don't believe they will phone at all, keep asking at other houses till you are sure at least one call has been made. Shops and offices are used to strangers coming in and are security conscious, so they will readily phone for you.

Tell until someone believes you and you get help
Quite a lot of children and their parents have now learnt this important Stay Safe message. Stay Safe also teaches that bystanders or witnesses should stop and/or report any abuse.

Scream
Ideally it should be enough for someone to scream or to shout 'Help! Help!', but people do not always respond to

such calls. Why not? Because they have been taught not to 'get involved'; because they believe that if you rush in you may do more harm than good and get hurt yourself; because a lot of screams are not connected to attacks; because 'Please help me' has been used many times to lure the unsuspecting person into a secluded spot to be mugged, robbed and worse; because many people, when they see someone who looks distraught or is screaming, in a wild state or in a state of collapse, assume that person is a drug addict, mentally ill or very drunk, and therefore dangerous and to be avoided; because they may assume that it's a joke or prank; because most people hate to be labelled a 'busybody'. As for phoning for the police/gardaí, there are a few people who would never bring in the gardaí, because where they live it is not 'the done thing'. Others hate phoning the police because the voice at the other end of the line often sounds cold and suspicious as a result of so many hoax calls.

In other words, people are not so much selfish and hardhearted as anxious to avoid trouble and unsure what to do for the best. This being the case, clear guidelines of information and advice can make a big difference, but only if enough people accept them. It is difficult to arrange for these to be taught in schools. One reason is that both teachers and parents emphasise independence rather than interdependence (*see* Independence).

More examples of how bystanders can help to stop bullying can be found in books, including *Kidscape: Stop Bullying*. Books, films, TV and videos often show people handling bullying problems – discussing these can help a group to consider which methods seem safe, sensible and effective and therefore suitable to adopt. In other words, there are many sources of skills worth acquiring; make it a policy to look out for these, to identify them, discuss them and practise them. Most people like doing the right thing but they need to feel they are competent to do it, and to believe that it is the right thing to do.

(*See also* **Acronyms – Sages.**)

A CaB Gets Started
'Take a CaB to a better life!'

IN NOVEMBER 1983, a Campaign against Bullying, CaB, was founded by Vivette O'Donnell in response to tales from every part of Ireland relating shocking events of violence and destruction which had occurred over the Hallowe'en period. The word 'bully' was the one in current use for the younger perpetrators of mischief, so 'bullying' seemed the right term for the behaviour of someone who was being a bully. It was clear that to tackle bullying successfully required the cooperation of virtually everybody. To gain this cooperation it was necessary to alert people to the problem and to suggest how it might be tackled. CaB therefore, set out to provide information and advice with the aim of reducing the incidence of bullying; it turned out that this often gave a welcome support to those affected by bullying. So what CaB has done has been to rouse, inform and support. CaB's first two leaflets are reproduced here. The first dates from November 1983 and the second from January 1984.

CaB Advice (Original Leaflet 1983)
Campaign against Bullying. Mrs. S. V. O'Donnell. Tel. 2887976
1. Be very watchful and protective. Don't allow your children to go anywhere that is likely to be dangerous.
2. Stop any form of bullying that concerns your children as soon as you observe it.
3. Believe your child enough to investigate and/or protect when the child says someone has bullied them.
4. NEVER GIVE IN TO A BULLY. GET HELP. Bullies pick on nearly everyone, but concentrate on the weak. Children should try to get a parent or friendly adult or teacher to deal with bullies, but if there is not time to alert an adult, a group of, say, six children, or teenagers,

attacked by two bullies is clearly safer if they stay in a tight group and defend themselves than if they scatter and it becomes two bullies against one member of the group. Screaming or blowing a police whistle helps to attract adult help.

5. When you have other people's children in your house or garden to play with your children, take care to supervise them closely and get to know them and gently correct their faults.

6. Impress upon children that hypocrisy is a vice. One may remain silent and one should be discreet but never tell lies.

7. Persuasion and loyalty, like hammers, are effective tools which can be used to build and to destroy, depending on intent. When the occasion arises, a relevant few words on the side of decency, integrity and high moral standards can have a very good effect in the long run. Although, among teenagers, these words may meet with outward derision, they often sink into the heart to good effect later. Good people need loyal friends too.

Campaign against Bullying   CaB

Never give in to a bully
They give chase if you don't stand your ground
A bully prefers easy meat to destroy
And picks on the timid and weak to annoy
So, never give in to a bully
They'll get worse if you don't stand your ground.
Never join up with the bullies
They will make you do things you don't like
To stay in their gang you must bully and jeer
And lie to your parents and steal, fight and fear
Both all decent folk and the bullies
Who make you a child you don't like.

CaB Information (Original Leaflet 1983)
Humans can be regarded on three levels:–

1. Physical – they have a body and observable behaviour e.g. reactions to stimulus – like iron filings but more complicated. Feelings such as awareness, pleasure, pain.

2. Mental/Intellectual – they have a brain and a mind and can think, reason, plan. Feelings as above plus anticipation, fear, anger, contempt, disappointment, joy ...

3. Spiritual/character and personality/soul – the spirit, awareness of God, conscience, aesthetic sense, love. Denial of these implies dead or half dead spiritual side. When these go wrong totally you have satanic, evil wickedness.

So, people are at risk from attack on their persons, on their minds, and on their characters/personalities/souls. People of great strength of character, like saints and martyrs, can endure physical and mental torture without damage to their characters/personalities/soul. Even so, they suffer if attacked by forms of physical or mental cruelty. Everyone suffers under such attack. Also, as Christians we must remember that anyone is at risk of being corrupted just as there is hope for everyone to be saved. We are all vulnerable, especially children under ten years of age who are comparatively small, ignorant and inexperienced. Parents can protect them more successfully if they know what forms attacks will take and what counter measures have best results. Here is a list of examples, some of which cause a great deal of distress and all of which have happened in this area, i.e. both bully and victim belong to the area. These are widespread and I recommend a big effort to stop even the minor forms of bullying.

1. *Physical Methods.*
   (a) Pushing and bumping, either obviously on purpose or seemingly accidentally.
   (b) Grabbing of victim or victim's possessions.
   (c) Stealing and/or destruction of victim's possessions.
   (d) Kicking and punching, including kicking between legs.
   (e) Knocking down on to the ground.

(f) Startling cyclists into accidents by suddenly jumping out.

(g) Throwing of eggs, stones, sticks ... at victim.

(h) Hitting with weapon, e.g. stick.

(i) "Telefono" (which can cause loss of hearing) and possibly other torture methods.

2. *Mental Cruelty.*

(a) Jeering, mocking, name-calling.

(b) Tale-telling that is true but unnecessary.

(c) Tale-telling that is false i.e. lies.

(d) Sowing seeds of doubt as to whether victim is loved by parents/friends.

(e) Sending to Coventry, i.e. no one even says "Hello" to victim.

(f) Saying things like: "I won't be your friend", "No you can't play with us", "If you want to play with me you can't play with her", "I won't let you come to my birthday party". i.e. making victim feel a friendless outcast.

3. *Character attacks* – spoiling the character and breaking victim's relationship with loved ones, especially with parents.

Form of method: If you want to play with us and be our friend, you will have to join "our gang". To join our gang you must do this (one or more of the following):-

(a) buy something you've been forbidden to buy, e.g. a ten-year-old buys a cigar or a six-year-old buys a box of matches;

(b) must steal from parents and buy for group: crisps, biscuits ... i.e. O.K. things; forbidden things;

(c) must steal from parents (or others) and give the money direct to gang/group funds or leader;

(d) lie to parents – deceive in any way, e.g. girls pretending to visit friends and sleeping rough;

(e) disobey parents, e.g.: by going to places or with people not permitted; by using foul language; by lighting unsupervised bonfires; by breaking windows especially of schools; by writing on walls; by fighting without provocation; by cheating; by bullying or watching bullying instead of getting it stopped.

People are cut to the quick by betrayal, i.e. when someone they thought was their true friend turns out to be not only false but even ready to be an enemy. Some friendships break up when tastes change or there comes a conflict of right and wrong or bullies make prolonged effort to break the friendship.

Examples :

1. 'You may keep this rubber, Anton.' 'Thank you, Dimitri.' Later: 'Look, everyone! Anton stole my rubber!' 'But you gave it to me, Dimitri. Remember?' 'Liar.' 'I thought you were my friend?' 'Not now, I'm not.' 'Nor I yours.'

The others don't know which to believe, thus straining relationships all round. Usually the innocent accused is not believed because too shocked to cope.

2. 'We used to be good friends, Kara, and enjoy chess and charades.' 'That is baby stuff, Freda. Do grow up.' 'But I don't want to smoke, drink, sample drugs, make risqué jokes, deceive my parents, do badly at school ...' End of friendship?

Not everyone wants to join an organised club such as school societies/Scouts/Guides or sports teams. But if all one's friends have drifted off to a bad set, one has only the choice of joining such a "safe" club or being a bit of a loner. Many, many children are loners, and that is quite all right if they have happy homes and plenty of camaraderie with their parents and siblings. Sometimes a new friendship will be formed through the many contacts made at school so one isn't necessarily a loner for long. It is very much better than joining, for companionship, a group that you hold in contempt because you gradually find that contempt for the others beginning to include yourself and self-contempt is a sad and dangerous thing which often leads to alcoholism and drug-taking. Everyone needs solid, genuine self-respect (the worst thing about unemployment is if it leads to loss of self-respect. In a recession such a loss is irrational, but it can happen.) Children may lose self-respect if they are doing badly at school because they are inattentive and neglect their homework. They are generally happiest when they know they are behaving properly.

General Notes

1. If you approve of CaB, please let me know.

2. If you feel an item should be added to the information lists, please let me know.

3. If you need help or advice such as members of CaB might be able to give, please contact either me or your nearest or any "friendly house".

CaB January 1984. Second leaflet.

1. What is bullying? Some dictionary definitions can clarify this matter. A bully is a quarrelsome, swaggering, cowardly fellow who terrorises or threatens those weaker than himself. The bully subjects his victim to abuse. He(she) abuses his(her) victim. To abuse is: to harm, ill-treat, injure, oppress, persecute, revile, victimise, violate, wrong.

Some opposites (antonyms) are: to cherish, benefit, protect, respect. From the victim's point of view, if the abuse caused distress, it was bullying. From the perpetrator's side, if the abuse was intended to cause distress, then it was bullying.

Teasing and good-natured funning, taken in good part, are not bullying. If teasing causes unintended distress, a quick and genuine apology puts all to rights. However trivial the teasing words or actions seem to an observer, they are deliberate, unkind bullying if they make the victim miserable.

2. Is a child ashamed of being bullied? Usually, yes! A child craves praise and popularity and associates unkindness with faults. To be told, 'Don't be a baby!' or 'They were only funning' or asked, 'Why won't they play with you?' or 'Have you no friends?' contributes to this unreasonable shame. It is bullies who should feel ashamed. Among the eminent and much loved people who have complained that they were bullied as school children are CS Lewis, Patrick

Campbell, Sir Laurence Olivier and Sir Ralph Richardson. Being bullied as a child does not indicate that the person is weak, unattractive or lacking in a sense of humour. In fact, a popular, gifted child arouses a bully's jealousy and by the use of lies and intimidation, the unchecked bully can do a great deal of damage to the victim.

3. Why have a campaign against bullying? The purpose of this campaign is to reduce the incidence of bullying and to minimise the ill-effects of bullying. Bullying is a serious nationwide problem. Life will be pleasanter if the campaign is effective. Bullying is a form of injustice and we have a moral duty to campaign against injustice.

Bullying and its attendant fear and distress stunt a child's growth. Adults have a duty to children to establish an atmosphere conducive to the full development of their potential. Bullying can lead children to drink, drugs, crime and premature death. The state 'cherishes all the children'. To cherish is to encourage, protect, nurture.

4. What about children's need to join a peer-group? Firstly, there is some confusion about what that means. The peer-group is often taken to mean 'All the kids who play outside on the street where you live'. A peer-group is a group of 'equals', i.e. companions, associates and rivals joined in a group because of similar interests or like-mindedness. A bully-gang is a peer-group where being a bully is a principal element of the like-mindedness. Bully-gangs are pernicious in their effects on their own members (e.g. playing dangerous 'don't be chicken' games) and in their effect on other peer groups, which they, as bullies, set out to torment and if possible to destroy, e.g. by picking on members of peer groups such as Scouts, ballet kids, young musicians etc. Children who enjoy playing together are in a good peer-group. Children who drag each other down are not. Any peer-group expects some conformity from its members – chess clubs, surgeons colleges, rugby teams etc. have obvious expectations associated with the members' activities. A group that goes in for shoplifting and foul language expects all members to do likewise. Children have a strong desire to gain acceptance in the nearest peer-groups. As with other desires, this one needs carefully judged control. If a local or school peer group has virtually nothing to recommend it, the child must resist the urge to join it. Let free choice rather than random chance, parental guidance rather than bully pressure, determine the activities and groups which children join.

The urge to gain acceptance by 'the group' is so great that children are easily persuaded to steal to gain membership.

The desire and determination to make all group members conform is so great that appalling pressure and deceit is readily used for this end. For example a member of very good character will be tricked by an invitation to a 'coffee and buns' party which, when she turns up, she discovers to be an 'alcohol and . . .' binge.

Loyalty to the group is usually supposed to override other loyalties. A teacher, Father Peter Moran, puts it very well: 'Even in the relatively sheltered atmosphere of our school, here, the strongest influence on our pupils seems to be their awareness of how their fellow pupils will react to anything: "peer-group pressure" as it is called', and, 'Even quite young children create a kind of "alternative ethic" to run parallel with the standards imposed by for example, school rules.'

5. *Children can be very cruel.* In young children the cruelty is mainly because they are young and therefore ignorant and inexperienced, and because they are children and therefore thoughtless and impulsive. Teaching and training and living should remove the causes, 'ignorance' and 'inexperience' by giving knowledge and experience; and the causes 'thoughtlessness' and 'impetuosity' by giving control, moral standards, courtesy, consideration, polite manners, understanding.

If a child's experience is of being left to get on with other kids as best he can, and if he is unlucky and the other kids are more than usually stupid, ignorant and unkind, and their bad behaviour is unchecked so that bullying seems to win, and bullies intimidate people who might be expected to control and deal with them, and if people are seen to rally round the bully when he is in trouble from decent folk but are not seen to rally round a victim of bullies, then the child is not receiving the necessary and proper training for becoming an adult, who lives by, and helps others to maintain, high moral standards, high standards of good behaviour, justice, law and order, protection of the innocent but weak, etc.

If one's reading is very wide, then the reading of a little pornography will certainly not warp or corrupt one's character or personality. If one's experience includes both good things and bad things, both happiness and sadness, vigour and sickness, kindness and cruelty, with more of all the good and happy things than of the sad and bad ones, then the little bits of bad will not harm one's character and personality. If one reads only porn, then one will be unduly influenced by it. If one experiences only unkindness, crude speech, or neglect, ditto. It takes a lot of good to counterbalance a little bad in one's personal life; this applies most of all to children because their youth and natural yearning to conform with their peer-groups, and to be the same as the other kids of their age, make them particularly vulnerable.

Classroom Management

'Teaching is the process of arranging things so that learning can happen.' Jack Hodgins.

THE FOLLOWING are some CaB thoughts on the important subject of classroom management. These have been found to be very important and effective in countering bullying.

Justice is important whatever your age. To children under the age of twelve, it is of paramount importance. A child's greatest indignation can be heard in the words, 'That's not fair.' Children simmering with resentment are not in the right frame of mind for learning. It is not enough for the teacher to be fair; the teacher must be *seen* to be fair, and to establish fairness among the pupils.

It is easier to have fairness if there is **openness**, and it is easier to have openness in an atmosphere where everybody shows courtesy, consideration and respect to everybody else. It is important that the children see the need for a teacher to be in charge to organise what is going to be studied, to give the necessary commands and instructions, and to take the necessary decisions. The students should see the teacher as someone who makes it possible for them to learn and achieve by setting their goals, showing how to reach them, guiding them along the way and helping them over their stumbling blocks:

'How are you getting on?'

'I'm stuck.'

'I would do this because ...'

'I still don't get it.'

'Look at it another way. Suppose ...'

'I can't get the hang of it – what am I doing wrong?'

'It won't work because ... you have to do this like this and then – see, now you have it. Now remember what you did to get it to work – that's right.'

The teacher is leader of the expedition, co-ordinator of the project, producer of the show, but she or he is also an adult friend and helpmate. This makes the teacher a great role model, and this can be reinforced by teacher and pupils all playing every part.

The teacher's **example** is of paramount importance. When the teacher *listens actively* to a pupil, the pupils learn how to be attentive listeners to both the teacher and to each other. This is reinforced by the occasional talk on the importance of listening skills. When the teacher acts as *mediator* in a dispute it helps the pupils to learn mediation skills to resolve conflict. When the teacher bothers to *'follow the leader'* very exactly, the pupils see how a good team member follows instructions. When they are put in the position of leader the pupils will, of course, model themselves on the teacher to some extent.

However, example is never enough; **precept** is absolutely essential. But a few words pointing out one or two things every so often builds up over time into a body of knowledge more effectively than a single long lecture covering every aspect of a topic. A good teacher will point out the things that pupils obviously don't know and that they most need to know, but will never make the pupils ashamed of their ignorance. By the time they leave school the pupils will, with good teaching, be competent, educated and sufficiently knowledgeable to be able to find out for themselves what they need to know, having learned from their teachers the research methods necessary.

A good teacher will **never assume** that pupils know things which they have not been taught. She or he will either elicit from them what they know without making them feel small because of their errors and ignorance, or teach everything from scratch, covering the ground quickly until it is clear that they need to slow down. The latter is quicker and easier for everyone, especially in a subject like mathematics.

Pupils can be **motivated** to learn by the teacher making sure they make progress, praising them and showing approval for achievements and progress. It is a great help if pupils notice that they enjoy mastering skills and achieving results. When they become reluctant to exert themselves to learn, they can be encouraged by pointing out that, for example, learning to walk was hard but they are glad they persevered – it is the same with learning to read and so on. A reward system of gold stars and class treats also works wonders.

Peer-tutoring – that is, encouraging pupils who have mastered something to tutor those who have not yet grasped it – will help to **reinforce** what they learn. Cooperation as well as competition can be encouraged by forming study-groups which cooperate in learning and practising, and in project work – written or artistic. Study groups are useful at all stages of education, especially at university level. Working as a member of a team is the norm in the work-place, so it makes sense to prepare for that at school with cooperative learning and problem-solving, brain-storming and discussion sessions in the classroom.

There is little chance of bullying when everyone is involved in activities that develop healthy relationships of respect, cooperation and helpfulness; where no one is scorned, humiliated or excluded; where everyone takes turns to be the leader - the one in charge and therefore the centre of attention - on a regular basis; where everyone is a team player and a member of a group. If you are a teacher, don't let anyone sneer, 'Imagine not knowing that (or how to do that).' Remind them that nobody knows everything, and that we can all learn from each other.

Make it normal for them to teach each other, from Infants class upwards. They enjoy it, it saves you work and they learn the lessons better – as well as learning how to pass on skills such as plaiting, doing and undoing buttons, tying laces and bows and, later, reading, playing musical instruments, dancing, sports skills et cetera. Keep making it clearly understood that 'you must know it before you can teach it', and check that what is taught is taught correctly.

Reassure children that, as they grow older, they will master skills which at first they find impossible. This applies just as much to fifteen-year-olds at Junior Certificate level – if they have at least average intelligence, then they could, with hard work, good teaching and plenty of study, eventually take any subject at Higher Level in the School Leaving Certificate examinations. It is a matter of their choice which subjects they will study and when they will study them.

Teenagers sometimes waste several years at school learning nothing, because they don't believe they have the ability to learn. The fact that many of these kids pass the exams later as mature students proves that this notion is usually mistaken. This crippling loss of confidence is often caused by bullying in primary school or early in secondary school. The techniques described in this chapter, of motivation, building on achievement, peer-tutoring, group cooperative learning, practice at being a leader and at being a member of the team being led, at being performer and at being audience, at being soloist or member of an ensemble, can prevent both the bullying and the waste.

On the other hand, if you start by dividing classes of five-year-olds into 'the fast readers', 'the average readers' and 'the slow readers', say that everything a pupil does must always be 'all your own work'; if you forbid any teaching of pupils by pupils and instead have competitions where one person wins the first prize and tests where some pupils always score less than 50 per cent, then instead of building self-esteem, self-confidence, academic ability and life skills, you will encourage the belief that people are winners or losers, and you will perpetuate the problem of bullying and underachieving in schools.

Now for some specific bullying problems and suggestions for what could be done to deal with them.

Remedial Classes
In some schools none of the other children will play with those in the remedial class, and bullying frequently occurs. Not all schools have a separate remedial class. Instead, children with academic or other problems have a couple of

sessions per week with the remedial teacher. This may be an individual session or a group session for several children with the same weak subject, such as spelling or fractions. Peer-tutoring greatly increases the help given to a child who is not up to the class standard in some subject. It also ensures the interaction of children who do with those who don't need remedial help. In many cases a child who is weak in one subject is strong in another, and will sometimes be a tutor as well as receiving tuition. This works well to avoid inequality and discrimination.

Teaching is always a rewarding learning experience, and all children benefit from tutoring. If the school structure does not permit this, it may be possible to arrange activities for several classes together with the remedial class. Suitable activities are some sports, lots of games, concerts, dance lessons, sing-songs and tightly organised parties where the children, under close supervision, set up food, drink, decorations, with lots of balloons, music, tricks, ice-breakers, games, party-pieces and some dance activity. Having cooperated with the remedial class on the preparation, all the children join them for the party. Some videos are fun for a wide range of age and ability. Story-telling and clowns would be fun for all. Once the children have been organised so that they mix pleasantly together and have shared experiences, prejudices will be weaker and they may be prepared to mix and play together in the schoolyard at break-time.

School fund-raisers such as fetes, fairs, cake sales and fashion shows also give opportunities to help the classes mix.

Safety and Playground Roughness

In some schools the children are very rough in the playground and careless about safety. These two problems can be tackled together by organising a visit from, for example, the Red Cross Schools Officers. These will teach safety skills and first aid, and will help organise class safety squads who take responsibility for reducing the number of accidents by preventive measures such as checking that people's shoelaces are tied and that nobody runs on the stairs.

After the visit, a class discussion will allow the pupils to say what they don't like about what happens in the playground, and what they would prefer. Then, with the teacher's help, they can draw up a class charter of playground rules which they all agree to keep. This charter will supplement the school rules, which may not go into much detail about what is acceptable behaviour in the playground. It should be written out as a poster and signed by everyone in the class.

The teachers could teach the children suitable games, and play with them to establish the appropriate rules and behaviour. The playground can be painted to look nicer, to separate quiet strolling areas from boisterous games areas, and to lay out hopscotch and other games ready for play. If there is a wall, the parents or local DIY might donate paints, and the children, with the help of some teachers, parents or art-college students, could paint a mural.

All these constructive, creative, organised activities are directly opposed to pointless rough behaviour, and directly work to stop bullying conduct getting a hold in the playground.

Fighting

'Every break time, all the boys thump and kick each other and knock each other down on the ground. Even my friend, the day he came back to school after his operation, had his arms twisted behind him and was flung on the ground and pounded, thumped and kicked. But he won't tell anyone, especially not his parents, who keep saying he's a weakling and has got to toughen up.'

'What about the teachers?'

'I told the teachers. The teachers say boys are always fighting.'

Deliberate fighting is different from playground roughness. Some school rules say quite clearly that fighting, kicking and punching are forbidden. They emphasise that these are serious offences, and that the penalty for a serious offence is suspension. When stated so clearly, these rules are obeyed.

A few other points:

- Don't put a child into only one category, for example 'good with their hands'.
- Value difference and tolerate disability – and deviation, if necessary, up to a point.
- Teach self-assessment and use the magic of the peer group to good purpose.
- If a child unwittingly annoys you by their behaviour, fix this without causing awkwardness of any sort, using techniques you would employ if you were dealing with an adult you liked who was also senior to you. The children will learn very useful techniques by observing you, and everyone will benefit from the tact they acquire in this way.
- Some bright children get up to mischief when they are bored. Make sure the children always have plenty to be busy with in between the lessons that should have their full attention.
- Make it clear that you think we should all be willing to help others and should feel responsible for others' safety, welfare and happiness, their good health, education and right to justice.
- Help the children to have joy and to appreciate beauty.
- Develop their sense of humour. You might consider using my rule in class: 'You may laugh at yourself or at me, if I slip up, but not at each other's mistakes.' Given that safeguard, you can recommend a robust sense of humour. As Ian Hislop observed, 'There is a certain callousness about satirical comedy ... but attacking vice, folly and humbug is fine.'
- If you are honest in a matter-of-fact way about making mistakes, having a headache, feeling a bit tired or having a sore throat, it is easier for the children to relate to you; they will feel more at ease and will show sympathy instead of taking advantage of the fact that you are under the weather.

- A pleasant atmosphere can be generated by playing music for a few minutes at various times during the day. If the class is cold and sluggish some teachers get them to do physical jerks such as jumping on the spot while chanting things, like grammar, that they should know by rote. Some teachers tell the class to sing a song like 'One Man Went to Mow' while they are out of the room for a minute. Some make the classroom more welcoming by introducing a pleasant smell like fresh coffee, bread, popcorn, pot-pourri or aromatherapy oils warmed on a nightlight burner. Some stock up the class library with cartoon books like *Garfield*. Some cut jokes out of newspapers and pin them on the class noticeboard. Many pupils are happy to keep a vase or two filled with flowers to brighten the room.

- If you are landed with a very disruptive class, get help from colleagues, and send for parents without delay. Don't let a discipline problem get a chance to develop.

- Discuss with the children what rules they think would be appropriate for their class. Then draw up a class charter, similar to the playground rules, which the pupils agree to and sign. Let the children suggest suitable penalties for infringement of the rules on the class charter. These will be too severe. Come to a satisfactory compromise and write that up also and have it signed.

- It is worth while to put time and effort into sorting out problems in September, so that the rest of the school year is relatively stress-free. That way the class will achieve more, there will be little bullying, if any, and you will not be stressed out by May or June.

- Finally, be assertive about what you want when talking to your principal and your colleagues about your class and your classroom. It goes without saying that you will be reasonable and cooperative, and will arrange matters with good sense, imagination and initiative. From one teacher to another, 'May your teaching hours be golden!'

Course Against Bullying

Detailed Daily Timetable for Bullying Course

THIS CaB course was designed in 1993 and conducted in that year and in 1994. The course was one of many recognised by the Irish Department of Education as in-service training for National (primary) School teachers. To be approved by the Department of Education, a course must satisfy several requirements. One of these is that the topic of gender equity, equality for males and females, must be included, either as one session (or module) or as an integral part of everything covered (the permeation approach). For gender equity there should be no discrimination on the grounds of sex or marital status. Bullying includes harassment and unfair discrimination on any grounds, including these.

The CaB will not be running this summer course again. However, as it was well received and much appreciated by those who attended it, I include here this summary. Anyone who wishes to use it when planning a course of their own is very welcome to do so.

Day 1
The course begins with a video which shows children, parents, teachers and others talking about bullying incidents, the effects of bullying, and ways of tackling the healing of victims and the reform and rehabilitation of bullies. The video also shows how to react to some kinds of bullying in order to counter them quickly and successfully, and how to develop an atmosphere or ethos in which bullying, though it may appear, cannot flourish or grow.

After the video, the students take part in a workshop, during which they write an essay entitled 'An Example of Bullying I Have Witnessed'. The lecturer gives the CaB's definition of bullying: 'Bullying is abuse which causes only distress in the victim and gives gratification and power to the bully.' The other definitions are also given. Causes, signs and diagnosis of bullying are dealt with as fully as possible. (Computer disks or printed notes will be given out on Day 5.)

In the second part of the afternoon students learn two folk-dances – Svensk Maskerade Marches (for pairs/couples) and Formation Skips. The steps are simply walking (for the first dance) and skipping (for the second). The music is lilting, and both boys and girls find these dances fun; socially they learn to dance together formally but not stiffly. Even with adults, problems such as fear of looking a fool, reluctance to hold hands with a partner, distrust of a group lest the movement become too wild, reluctance to exercise, reluctance to obey the beat of the music et cetera, will appear at first, as does the common feeling that men don't dance. Hopefully, by the end of the week, every participant will enjoy the eight folk-dances to be taught.

Day 2

The lecture deals with ways of preventing bullying, of which the school code of discipline is the first and most important. Detailed codes of discipline are described, as are class contracts, where the children make up their own class code to supplement the school rules. Some cures for bullying situations are also covered.

The essay to be written in the afternoon is 'An Example of a Bullying Incident Successfully Dealt With'. The class essays add to the already considerable body of research on bullying in Ireland.

The lecture is on the subject of class and playground management, including the importance of boys and girls being allowed to perform duties, play games and learn subjects sometimes thought of as being only or mainly the prerogative of one sex.

The folk-dances for Day 2 are Black Forest from China and Troika from Russia. The first is charming but not tiring, and Troika is very easy, very energetic and requires good cooperation to perform properly. Bullies spoil Troika by preventing the successful completion of the dance, and by pushing, pulling and bumping; bully-victims spoil it by being slow and obstructive.

Day 3

The lecture is on how to inform children about bullying while teaching various subjects. The need for rules is seen in maths; emotions, imagination, stories come into the English syllabus; motivation, power, rebellion are important in history; pollution, exploitation, rich resources occur in geography; the scientific method, experiments, pragmatic and logical thinking, research and questionnaires, tests, evidence et cetera are important in science.

The essay task is to draft an anti-bullying lesson in subject context.

The afternoon lecture is on counselling, contracts and therapy, whether for a whole class, a small group or one-to-one. Contracts help children to take responsibility for their actions. Therapy will aim to solve problems and raise self-esteem.

The folk-dances on Day 3 are Greek: Sirtaki (sideways and three hops back) and Servikos. Both these dances involve keeping in line, holding the arms so that your hands are on the shoulders of the people on either side of you – and also doing spectacular (but simple) solo steps. The dances encourage healthy competition at demonstrating ability. They give girls the opportunity to show they can jump as high as boys and that they have as much stamina; and give boys the chance to show they can be nimble and have fine control.

Day 4

Lecture on morale, disillusionment, stress and burnout. Children who have problems of their own can find that the suffering and injustice they see on the news every day makes them feel hopeless about the future. This must be put in perspective. It helps if fair play is the norm at school and if interesting rather than sad or terrible news stories are discussed. Balance is important.

Stress and burnout are only too common among teachers, and the signs of these are given, as well as some of the best up-to-date advice. The importance of convalescence and the danger of ME (myalgic encephalomyelitis) will be mentioned.

The essay centres on making an anti-bullying lesson from an article in the previous day's newspapers or magazines.

The lecture is on cooperation from parents with regard to the prevention or cure of bullying. Obviously, if the ideals and standards observed at home are similar to those upheld at school, and if both are good, parent–school relationships will be friendly. Even if a child is unfortunate as regards home background or circumstances, she can learn to conform happily with the prevailing ethos of the school.

The folk-dances for Day 4 are the Latin-American Conga, very popular in Ireland as elsewhere, and Fado Blanquita from Portugal – a dance which involves both full-circle and partner sections, and which is mainly sociable, though the steps are stylish in the second and third sections. It is a dance of the type where perfect accuracy of step-execution is not at all important, but where a party atmosphere is. Many children find it hard to behave in a fitting manner at parties; Day 4's dances help them to have fun and be light-hearted as part of a group.

Day 5

In the morning there is a discussion reviewing the week's topics. CaB notes/disks are given to the class. In the afternoon there is a lecture on encouragement, happiness and achievement. When people enjoy achievement they are eager to work for more. Praising progress is easy and effective. Teaching children to be glad of any progress they make, rather than comparing their standard too closely with that of others, helps. Healthy competition helps too – as soon as one child masters something, the next ten suddenly find they can do it too. If there is a good class atmosphere, those who know how to do something may be able to teach the others, laying a basis for forming study groups at second and third level.

Bullying

It is very hard for bullying to start, let alone continue, in such a class. Peer pressure in these circumstances works for everyone's good. The recurring problem is jealousy, which can quickly lead to bullying unless the subject is openly discussed in class lessons as a matter of course, and also whenever it is spotted – but as tactfully as possible.

One approach is through different kinds of beauty in flowers, different personal tastes, different kinds of music, different styles of art, dress, dancing et cetera. The eight folk-dances are revised towards the end of the day, and the notes and music-tapes for these are given out to everybody.

Custom

'When in Rome do as the Romans.'

EVERYONE is accustomed to what counts as good manners, firstly in the family home where they grew (or are growing) up, secondly in the schools and other milieux where they mix. Children learn to be scandalised at any deviation from their code – or rather codes, for they often have a different code for every group they belong to, with consequent restraint or embarrassment when groups mix. Slagging about such differences is a common form of bullying.

Beautiful manners are always delightful, and disapproval and criticism are appropriate where there is abuse of any sort. Having said that, variety is the spice of life, and valuing ourselves and others includes valuing the many different variations on customs, accents, food, dress and so on.

It seems to me a great mistake to take offence where it is obvious that none is intended, and an even greater mistake to encourage children to do so. At the same time it is very important not to put up with something you greatly dislike without voicing any kind of protest; good-hearted people will not wish to distress you, and bullies must not be allowed to bully you.

It is wise to assume nothing, learn as fast as you can and remember that if a person from another household has, apparently unwittingly, broken one of your taboos, it is almost certain that they have kindly disregarded the many times that you have broken theirs.

Dance

DANCE helps children not to become bullies, and helps to rehabilitate the victims of bullying, but few people really know what dance is.

What Is Dance?

1. Dance is a performance art like music-making and acting. In one category one would put classical ballet (like *Swan Lake/Giselle*), classical music (like Mozart/Beethoven), classical plays (Shakespeare). In another one has folk dance, folk music, folk plays; and in yet others there are jazz, pop *et cetera*. An appreciation of dance teaches one to value diversity and variety, and discourages the intolerance of difference which is a feature of bullying behaviour.

2. Dance is a form of expression – like music it can be understood universally without need for translation. It can express every emotion and depict any situation/story, or it can be abstract. Because it's non-verbal there is no language barrier. This makes it ideal for integrating the remedial classes with the other classes in a school.

3. Dance is joy in moving – we jump for joy, we stretch with pleasure. Bullies are killjoys.

4. Dance is release (from stress, tension, restrictions) and freedom of expression. Dance can be a statement of identity: 'This is who I am' – a statement infinitely preferable to vandalism. Also, in dance one can play-act other characters and personalities.

5. Dance is recreation. Dance is fun.

6. Dance is exercise: *ceteris paribus*, it is safe, healthy, energetic exercise to music which is not boring but does promote grace and good posture. Someone who dances looks confident, which is a great help to avoid attracting bullies. Dance also exercises the brain, the memory and the emotions.

7. Dance has ideals and standards which are a clear measure for the dancer, preventing self-satisfaction and vanity but encouraging healthy pride in achievement. It is unlike competitive sports in that in dance there do not have to be losers.

8. Dance can be an enjoyable social activity, like singing round a campfire. If youngsters have plenty of enjoyable social activities, they are unlikely to resort to drink, drugs or violence.

9. Folk-dance lessons can be used to identify relationship problems and to establish desirable social interactions in a pleasant, enjoyable way. Ethnic dance is particularly useful to counter racism.

10. Dance is Universal. Dance is Movement. Dance is Life.

All professions can be the target of bullies – lawyers are attacked as sharks, journalists as hacks, builders as macho louts. Here we note that dance is bullied as a profession, and the reader may recognise that similar attacks are made on their own calling.

Dance as a profession is undervalued, even when considered in the contexts of art, recreation, healthy exercise or social skills. In fact dance is often called the Cinderella of the Arts, and with good reason. Cinderella is, of course, the archetypal innocent and virtuous victim of bullying; compared to her stepsisters she is poverty-stricken, overworked, slighted and neglected. Similarly, dance is poverty-stricken – and tends to receive the smallest allocation in Arts Council budgets. Any dancer will elaborate further!

Until recently, most men learned to dance social dances. At my own school in Scotland the boys as well as the girls learned to polka and waltz, and to dance the Dashing White Sergeant and the quickstep. However, even then there was prejudice against men who did ballet. And in spite of all the work for gender equality, the situation today is even worse – 'Real men don't dance.' (Men often claim that the dancing at discos and raves is partying, not dancing.) Although the current (1995) Irish Minister for Culture and the Arts, Michael D. Higgins, encourages the teaching of dance in schools to both boys and girls, unfortunately the prejudice against males who dance is so great that the only way to overcome it is to make dance a compulsory subject all through primary school.

Disability

THE easiest and most despicable form of bullying is cruelty which focuses on what makes a child obviously vulnerable. One would hope that children with a disability of any sort would be bullied less than their peers, but in fact the reverse is the case. One reason is the bullies' tenet 'victims deserve to be bullied'. The number suffering is huge, because temporary problems, such as squints, limps or specific learning difficulties, cause the affected children to be bullied, and by the time the initial problem is cured they have become long-term victims of bullying, with all its associated psychological ill-effects and stress-induced illnesses. One boy was still called 'Limper' and 'Cripple' ten years after his limp had been healed.

In ordinary schools a prevalent form of bullying is to call a child 'mental', 'header' or 'spastic'. Children with a disability or just out of hospital are often physically assaulted. Girls with a mental handicap are more likely to be sexually assaulted, and one comes across the attitude: 'Well, that is to be expected – perhaps she could be sterilised so that at least she does not get pregnant.' It is *not* to be expected.

Countering bullying involves developing attitudes of mind and norms of behaviour which make such conduct unthinkable. Everyone should play their part in this, especially the main educators of children: parents, teachers and children themselves.

Understanding Others
Most cruelty springs from fear, hate, jealousy, anger and humiliation. Few bullies face up to the hurt they are causing or have caused; if possible, they shift responsibility for the consequences of their actions on to others.

Children will not develop humanity just by picking it up

as they go along. They need precept and example, appeals both to the heart and the intellect. They need to build progressively on their experiences in order to become truly human, sensitive and compassionate. Empathy and fellow-feeling, a sense of justice and fair play, can be developed by everything we do, as well as through stories told in any form, including ballet and opera. It is particularly important to give children the vocabulary they need to express their feelings, because it will enhance both children's relationships and their academic work. This vocabulary should include words, fables, allegories, mime, movement, dance, music and artwork – even games and gardening. This increases the possibilities for expression and for understanding, for the greater development of the imagination and so for greatly enriched experience.

It is unfortunate that some parents try to give their children a wide range of experience but omit any attempt at character development. They hope or assume that the children will 'pick it up', but, without guidance, what is picked up is likely to be something trivial but eye-catching that other children comment on. For example, they will notice and talk about the costumes rather than the artistry or the themes of ballets, operas and plays, and about people's appearances and looks, rather than what they were actually talking about.

At the very basic level, children must be taught that it is shockingly wrong to be hostile to anyone because that person has a disability. Those with disabilities need to be taught assertiveness and communication skills so that they can forestall attacks with an assertive manner, and report any bullying incidents as quickly and clearly as possible. It is very difficult for a deaf child to cry out for help or shout 'No', but with time teachers do help them to follow the Stay Safe rules of 'Say no. Get away. Tell someone you trust'.

Sometimes work is done to build the inner confidence and self-worth of children with disabilities, but outward charm and assertiveness lessons are omitted. Some disabled people cannot bring themselves to ask for help, while others ask too aggressively, putting people off. Training in these skills is of fundamental importance, and when they are taught from a very young age, disabled children are bullied less rather than more often than the norm.

Nobody Is 100% Perfect

Because nobody is 'the best' at everything, everyone can, with effort, learn to understand disability and special needs. We need to be more open: many able-bodied people still recoil in horror if someone says, 'That's just one of my disabilities,' and try to reassure the disabled person that 'No, no, that's quite normal.'

Whether or not they have a disability or a bullying problem or both, some people are grateful for help, but can never bring themselves to ask for it unless forced to do so. Some others want to succeed on their own and may even resent help, even though they admit that it is to their advantage – despite the fact that it hurts their pride and causes them shame and embarrassment. Some concentrate on their goals and ask for all the help they can get to reach them. And a small minority ask for help because they want extra attention. This last group need to be taken aside for a little one-to-one chat, so that they understand what they've been doing and so that if they have a problem for which they need counselling, this can be arranged. Bullies always claim that their victims belong to this last group – a very hurtful jibe.

Kids who need remedial help are often bullied at school, although most schoolchildren need some remedial help at some stage. Generally the brightest and the weakest are the most likely to be given extra help. The brightest are encouraged to aim for the glittering prizes. The weakest have no choice in the matter. Usually kids get tutoring from siblings, parents, friends or relations. Sometimes they get private tutors or go to grinds, and some have remedial teaching provided at school. Those coached at home are often the most likely to scoff and sneer at those in remedial classes at school.

Bullying attitudes can be changed by taking every opportunity for children to develop healthy and helpful attitudes towards each other's learning, for example: by improving each other's skills by working in pairs or groups; by giving constructive criticism with help on offer; by always giving some praise where it is due; by admitting to having had difficulties in mastering some skills and by saying how these were overcome; and by always being encouraging. Unfortunately, as stated already in the sections on Achieving and Classroom Management, many children sneer at classmates who slip behind in any subject, and they work, not because they are motivated to learn, but because they fear that they'll be sneered at in their turn. Some even sneer at books, steps, tunes et cetera which they see as being suitable only for 'babies' or 'infants'. They may need to have it pointed out that even at university use is made of words like 'and' and 'the', which are in the infants' books, and of concepts like $1 + 1 = 2$; and even ballerinas do skips in classical ballet solos on stage.

Bullying of Those with Handicaps or Disabilities

The bullying of children with disabilities can be prevented, for children mostly do what they are told, and most of what they are told they hear from other children. Some adults, through their language or attitude, convey the message that disparaging remarks are in some way appropriate; some just make too big a deal about how great it is that this child has perfect sight, that one has supple limbs or another is always healthy, smart or nobody's fool. Some of these remarks suggest that the person with a problem deserves it, and families have been ostracised because a child was born autistic or malformed.

Given that some children have accepted that if you have red hair you deserve to be bullied (as Neil Kinnock remembers), it is no wonder they can be persuaded that a dyslexic child deserves to be called stupid.

Sometimes a child is bullied because the rest of the class feel jealous when the teacher says how brave he is after his operation, or how hard she has worked to learn to read. The moral is not that the teacher should avoid giving the child any praise and attention, but that the class should have lessons involving stories about jealousy so that they can recognise and overcome it.

Pupils in Transition Year, usually at about the age of fifteen or so, are sometimes introduced to people with disabilities, and gain insight and maturity as a result. However, insensitive little brats can do so much harm to vulnerable children that it is not satisfactory to leave this till they are over fourteen years old.

Effects of Bullying on People with Disabilities

Coping with a disabled family member puts a great strain on everyone in the family, and this strain can become intolerable if they have also to bear the effects of bullying: anger, stress, shame, blame and guilt. They feel discouraged and lose heart. The strain can cause marriages to break up and children to leave school, run away from home, and even kill themselves. Meanwhile, the effect on the bullies is to perpetuate cruel attitudes which will give no happiness to themselves, their colleagues, their workmates, their families or their neighbours. Sometimes victims' resentment smoulders to the point where they set out to kill the person who bullied them.

Conclusion

It is everyone's birthright to have zest for life, for picking up challenges and for overcoming difficulties. If at any time we have helped or inspired anyone, we have achieved much. Coping with a disability is difficult and daunting. So is tackling bullying. Coping with a disability takes courage and determination. So does tackling bullying. Laughter and humour are sanity-savers for those with disabilities. So are they for those tackling bullying. That's a lot of shared experience, empathy and fellow-feeling to be going on with – probably enough to guarantee success.

Eliminating Bullying:

A Cookbook of Recipes and Menus for Social Education

ELIMINATING bullying requires *prevention, intervention* and *changing attitudes* so that bullying becomes unthinkable. But how are we to achieve such healthy attitudes, such healthy relationships?

One of the main criticisms of anti-bullying booklets, lectures and meetings has been that 'There is nothing of practical use to me' – mirroring the messages sent to nutritionists: 'We don't want to hear that we need protein, fat and carbohydrates, vitamins, minerals, amino acids and trace elements; we want to be given menus and recipes and how to prepare them. We want cookbooks for maintaining good health, and cookbooks for restoring good health, and cookbooks for alleviating and minimising, rather than aggravating, the symptoms of illness.' There is now an abundance of cookbooks of every sort. Similar resources are available and more are being produced for those people involved in countering bullying (see resources lists).

Confucius said, 'Food is the first happiness.' Sharing first place, though, must be loving relationships. The child's first and foremost cook and social educator is usually its mother, with other family members, friends and professionals, such as child-minders and teachers, playing an increasingly important role. Being a mother or mother-substitute is the most difficult job there is. One reason for this is the frequent occurrence of the unexpected, the unprepared-for and the untrained-for, something which is not a feature of most jobs. Another reason is the inconsistent advice with which mothers are bombarded from all sides. Experts often disagree, and 'while doctors differ, patients die'. The platitude that 'mothers generally know what's best for their own child' is scant reassurance to anyone with powers of observation, or to one whose child is not thriving as well as expected. Some mothers have put more work into finding a solution to their child's problem than ever went into the research for a thesis or project.

Daily Staple Diets

Say yes if you possibly can, but if you say no, mean it – this is good advice in general. Rules of thumb like this are like a set of basic meals: easy, nourishing, economical and easily varied according to individual tastes or needs. Useful rules of thumb, proverbs and sayings, when discussed, give a shared foundation of attitudes and standards. Any that are pernicious, such as 'Flatter the fool and get work out of him', need to be exposed and denounced. Others, such as 'If you can't beat them, join them', need more discussion to decide whether they have any merit and, if so, under what circumstances.

Also worth discussion is the extent to which people live by these maxims and the results that follow. Can these be changed?

Teaching children to check whether something is true or untrue, and to make value judgements, are necessary ingredients in all our social education menus. Example: 'They don't appreciate the value of what you are teaching their children; they are using the school as a baby-sitting service.' Probably entirely true of some parents, partly true of many. Does it matter? To some extent, yes – children thrive on deserved praise, encouragement and appreciation. All families have to allow for diversity of tastes and interests. So a suitable reply would be, 'At least the children are being educated.'

Another example: a thirteen-year-old boy is crying his eyes out. His father asks what's wrong. The boy says several boys at school are calling him gay. His father says, 'First let's be clear – do you think you are gay?' The boy says, 'No, certainly not!' Sensible father says, 'That's what I expected you to say. Of course, you're not gay, and no one who knows you thinks you are, and that includes these bullies who are saying it to bully you. They try to bully all boys like that – girls too, believe it or not. It is abominable behaviour and unacceptable in any school. I will speak to the school principal about how contrary it is to the school's vaunted ethos. Next time try saying, "I bet you say that to all the lads", and remind yourself how stupid, pathetic and unoriginal they are, just copying the same old taunts bullies have used for decades, and lying as well.'

A well-meaning but occasionally stupid father, more used to talking than to listening, is liable to irritate his child by saying, 'Because if you are gay, your mother and I are tolerant, broad-minded people who can help you to come to terms with it and cope with the various difficulties etc.'

Anyone faced with a culinary disaster wants to know 'What went wrong and why?' The second example went wrong when the son didn't get the ideal response, because the father went on talking, instead of listening and then responding to what the son was telling him in words and in non-verbal expression of feelings, such as tone of voice. Most people make this kind of mistake when caught on the hop where they are emotionally involved. In certain highly charged circumstances people jump to conclusions and babble. Apologise and be forgiven, and call it a learning experience for us all.

Menus Combining Food and Social Education

The analogies of food and recipes can be used to explore many topics. Basic foods and basic ethics are similar for all humankind; therefore one can stress the humanity of all races and classes, and combat racism, classism, ageism and sexism, all of which are forms of bullying, abuse and injustice. From appreciating the similarities between the foods of different cultures, such as meat balls which are *frikadellars* to the Danish, *keftes* to the Greek and Lions' Heads to the Chinese, one can move to valuing diversity, and showing how variety enriches our experience. All can participate in discussions on food; here is something everyone, no matter what their IQ or their wealth, has in common. Progressing the discussion from food to customs, clothes, weather, folktales, qualities admired or despised, and all art forms, we can develop empathy and understanding, liking and compassion for others in the same school, the same region, the same world. All of this makes us a menu of nourishing, interesting and delectable dishes with 1,001 project possibilities.

Reacting to Bullying

Just as families hand down tried and tested dishes, they also hand down tried and tested methods for dealing with bullying:

- *instant tit-for-tat* – excellent unless it escalates, which it often does; so better to use
- *warnings* – 'Don't do that. I'll tell you once, I'll tell you twice, the third time you pay the (explicit) penalty';
- *the bristle factor* – takes various forms, all of them meaning, 'Unless I get a satisfactory explanation and apology, you are in big trouble for what you just did.' Answers like 'Whoops sorry, my mistake', 'It was an accident', 'I didn't mean any disrespect', 'It was just a joke – no offence intended' are usually accepted, more or less grudgingly depending on the situation;
- *ignoring, avoiding, saying the unexpected, quick wit or humour, change of subject and distraction* all work well unless the aggressor is further enraged by failure, frustration and humiliation. If anyone notices that someone is full of jealousy and bitter resentment, they should attempt to get help for that person, for example by alerting a school teacher, counsellor or parent. A group session for conflict resolution, where each person has the opportunity to vent their feelings and give their version of events, can clear the air;
- *nip the bullying behaviour in the bud* – if possible without causing hurt or humiliation. Humiliation rankles for ever. As much as possible, try to separate the behaviour from the person. At the same time, make them take full responsibility for their actions, point out the consequences of their actions and the even worse possible consequences of such actions – for example, 'Suppose she'd jerked and the knife had cut an artery; she could have died.'

Regular Meals

Order, routine, good habits, safety and emergency procedures form a framework for daily life. This framework need
not be rigid, and it can be changed according to need or
convenience. Homes need house rules and the security of
some definite expectations. So do institutions, communities,
societies, countries. At national level, people have the
Constitution and statute books, the law, the Department of
Justice. As has been said by politicians and Church leaders,
society is underpinned by family values. Leaders have been
less ready to acknowledge that family values can be under-
mined and eroded by their policies.

Schools are uniquely placed to help their community to
develop a good basic language, understood by all, and a
good basic set of rules, standards and ideals, common to all.
It is very much in schools' own self-interest to do so, as the
risk of arson, burglary and vandalism would be greatly
reduced, and both staff and students would enjoy working in
a safe and pleasant atmosphere.

Recipes for rules and contracts, and methods for conflict
resolution et cetera, can be found elsewhere in this book in
several chapters, including **Mediation** and **Workplace
Bullying.**

Individual Diets

Finally, allow for individuality. What is good wholesome
food for most people may be poison for others with allergic
reactions. If you can see that scorn and scolding are inappro-
priate responses to someone who comes out in hives when
they eat strawberries, it is clear that you should hesitate
before using them in reaction to those who are very shy or
cautious by nature, or as a result of some past experience.

When in doubt, find out. In the short term: if in doubt –
don't!

Fool

UNDER this heading there are two major forms of bullying:

- the bully tries to make the victim *feel* a fool,
  for example by exaggerating every mistake he makes;
- the bully tries to make the victim *look* a fool,
  for example by tripping him up. If the bully succeeds,
  the victim is devastated.

However, bullies can use other methods. 'You were excellent as the fool, but then you're a natural' is witty enough to be relished if said by a friend, but cruel if said by a bully.

Seeing this kind of behaviour, a teacher may try to protect the victim by saying, 'They are making a fool of you, lad. Don't do it.' The bullies may be asking the boy to show them some skill like playing the flute, say, but are laughing at his appearance when he plays. The bullies should be reprimanded for their ill manners. It may be this lad's policy to accede to a reasonable request, especially if it involves little effort and no discomfort – why not be obliging, rather than disobliging? True, sometimes, bullies will pretend among themselves that he's a puppet and they're pulling his strings, in which case he has his revenge – the last laugh.

Really, as always, it is the bullies whose behaviour deserves censure, the bullies who should be told, 'Don't do it!'. This will probably not alter their behaviour, but it is enough to make plain to them that they are being regarded with disapproval. It will stop them if they like to regard themselves as superior and as achievers. It does require a major shift in attitude for people to focus their attention on the bullies rather than on the perceived victim when there is a need for a change in behaviour. To encourage such a shift is a main aim of this book.

Games

GAMES are both antithesis and antidote to bullying. Games can be invaluable for distraction and to relieve boredom which might otherwise lead to bullying. They help to develop children's abilities to appreciate, discriminate, adapt, create, cooperate, communicate, learn, assess, exult and congratulate. They provide ways of resolving conflict, settling arguments, compromising and agreeing. Some decisions can be taken by majority vote, some by tossing a coin, drawing straws or throwing dice. This is better than forcing decisions by bullying aggression.

Many useful books of games and puzzles are available. Parents may need to learn a few for parties, wet holidays and when someone is sick in bed. Teachers could set as a project for their class that each pupil has to find a game and teach it to the class. Otherwise, children are unlikely to research new games and will stick with that tiny percentage – less than one per cent – of games which are currently fashionable with their peers.

Some children prefer adapting games so they can use their imagination and originality. Others are very conservative. It is valuable to develop creativity and the ability to adapt things to one's purpose and convenience: 'What can I do, with what I've got, where I am, now?' Many games like tag, chasing and football have almost unlimited versions. On the other hand, for many games, such as chess, it is essential to be able to play by the book and stick rigidly to the rules. But even chess has the variation Ultima. Over-conservatism is too limiting to be allowed. In the Action Transport programme it is suggested that only one version of each game be in any one school as this saves time, and school breaks are short. In general, however, we should never let the kids say that one version is the only right one. Do, however, insist that rules are agreed in full before play begins.

Here is a list of games which children of all ages can play, starting with those suitable even for those with movement restricted by illness, injury or lack of space. Many can be played by one person alone, but all can be played in the company of friends either alongside or interacting with each other:

TRADITIONAL GAMES: *Peep; One Potato, Two Potato; Pat-a-Cake; Clap Hands; Itsy-Bitsy Spider; Roundabout Ran a Wee Mouse; My Wee Jeanie's Pinafore; Where's Teddy?; Hunt the Thimble (or the slipper or the bar of chocolate); 'Guess what animal I am being. Miaou'; Can you balance a book/bottle on your head?; Keep the balloon off the floor; juggling; percussion band; I spy with my little eye.*

CARD, DICE AND BOARD GAMES: *patience; snap; cheat; Stop the Bus; nap; rummy; whist; bridge; vingt-et-un; poker; dice* – statistical probability, number of moves, who starts et cetera; *peg-board games – solitaire, Chinese checkers, Piquet; board games – Go, chess, draughts, Snakes and Ladders, Ludo, Monopoly, Mine a Million, Trivial Pursuit* and many others, such as *Cluedo.*

WORD GAMES: *Scrabble; hangman; crosswords; word searches; given these nine letters how many words can you make?; what word contains these three letters in this sequence?; adverb game, popular thirty years ago:* e.g.'"You remind me of The Venus de Milo," said Tom disarmingly'; *the poem game – Hinky Pinky* – a topic is written by one person, usually as a question, and given to another player who writes a poem in answer. First everyone writes a question then these are handed over and everyone writes a poem, time limit about twenty minutes. Those willing read them out; *lists* – everyone suggests things (not more than twenty) such as flower, comic, animal, singer, food, fruit.

Someone picks a letter and everyone writes down one of each thing starting with that letter. Repeat with new letter; *backronyms:* make new words for acronyms, for example CIA, Cuban Invasion Agency; *speak in titles:* players converse only in titles of songs, films, TV programmes, books; *start with next letter* – two players converse – each has to reply starting with a word that starts with the next letter in the alphabet, e.g. 'Good morning,' 'How are you?' 'I'm fine, and yourself?' 'Just grand. Where have you been?' 'Kingston – I ...'; *converse only in questions* – for example, 'How are you?' 'Why do you ask?' 'What's the matter?' The game of countering a question with a question is excellent practice for dealing with bullies who try to wrongfoot you with tiresome questions and comments, e.g. 'What do you mean?' Stronger, 'What do you mean by that?' Also used but not recommended, 'What is that supposed to mean?'

PICTURE GAMES: *jigsaws; tracings; rubbings; fashions; paper dolls; cartoons; spot the difference; scrap books; collages; noughts and crosses; drawing; painting; decorating; pavement chalks; murals; 3-D noughts and crosses.* Make your own cards, calendars, letterheads, logos, autographs. *Funny Pictures* – draw head, fold paper over so that head is invisible, pass on, draw body not knowing what head is, fold over, pass on, draw legs et cetera, draw feet et cetera. Delightfully absurd results; *Describe and Draw:* one player describes a photo or picture in a magazine, the others attempt to draw it from description alone – questions are allowed; *Submarines* – each player marks six submarines on a piece of paper. Take turns at dive-bombing them with a pencil (eyes shut). Game ends when one has lost all submarines.

PROBLEM-SOLVING GAMES: *maths puzzles; riddles; detective work* – following clues et cetera; *role-playing game books; video games* such as *Dungeon Master* and *Civilisation.*

BUILDING GAMES: *bricks; Lego; Meccano; take an old clock to pieces and put it together again;* use books and boxes et cetera to build forts, garages, towns and *fantasy worlds* – people them with toy figures.

COMBINATION: combine stories, dialogues, board games, puzzles and building ideas to create new games where imagination has free rein.

PARTY GAMES: *charades; improvisation* of scenes or songs in various styles such as soap, Shakespeare, Tom and Jerry, or hoe-down, love song, rock and roll, opera; *party host* – tries to guess which character the guests are playing; *dummy keyboard* – one player plays rhythm of a tune, the others try to identify it, winner plays next tune; *'Odd one out'* requires preparation, as does *The Fair* with lots of competitions set up such as throwing hoops, knocking skittles and other throwing and physical games; *memory games*, such as remembering all the objects on a tray, or strings of adjectives, each person adds one more adjective to the string; *spelling games* – each person adds one letter, but must have a real word in mind; *trains and statues* – small children love forming a train like a conga line and trotting along saying 'Chuff-chuff-chuff-chuff-chuff-toot-toot', changing leader at the party organiser's word. The ex-leader becomes the last carriage in the train; *dancing, both folk and disco* – ideal for older children who prefer a party organiser to show steps and arrange partners, lines, circles, squares, threesomes ...; *blowing bubbles*, a great favourite with little kids.

SPORTY GAMES: *snooker; darts; swingball; tennis; badminton; ping-pong; putting; golf; croquet; Donkey, Over the Mill; One-Two-Three a Leary; other bouncing-ball games; skipping games; hopscotch; pitch and toss; hop-step-and-jump; cricket; rugby; rounders; hockey; football; hurling; soccer; camogie; basketball; French cricket* – the aim is to hit someone's legs with a tennis ball while the person defends with a tennis racquet or cricket bat or anything handy; *skiing; riding; rock-climbing...*

KERBIES: bouncing a ball off the kerb of the pavement is very popular with Dublin kids but not with pedestrians, cyclists, car drivers or householders.

LET'S PRETEND – the all-time favourite is for an adult to be a monster for the children to sneak up on and be chased by. School version – kids creep behind the Wolf, saying, 'What's the time, Mr Wolf?' The wolf may say any time, but if s/he says, 'It's dinnertime,' the wolf will chase the kids. The one who's caught becomes the new wolf. The kids reach 'safety' if they get behind a set line, so the chasing is limited. There's a great number of other pretend games.

WATER GAMES: in the garden or at the beach or riverside.

WATER SPORTS: *sailing; surfing; scuba diving; swimming; water polo; fishing.*

MARTIAL ARTS: *tai-chi, kung fu, karate.*

OTHER: *fencing; polo; sky-diving; hot-air ballooning; gliding; bungee-jumping; kite-flying; ice skating; roller skating; ballroom dancing; radio-controlled model cars, boats, aeroplanes; anything that takes your fancy...*

Independence

'I SUPPOSE we are here for the high academic standards, but it is mainly to teach us to be independent. That's silly really, because we are all dependent on others; nobody is completely independent.'

This is a nine-year-old boy speaking about boarding schools. He's right. Nobody is completely independent or totally helpless. Even the hermit is dependent on the environment for air, food, water and shelter. Even the patient on the life-support machine is getting help. Even the new-born baby has power – her cry can summon food, warmth and comfort as she needs them.

Until recently we knew very little about bullying or what to do about it, and just said whatever our own parents and teachers had said. Now we have found out that some of these things were myths and bad advice, and that some of our problems as adults are the result of bullying which was not tackled well when we were children.

One of the mistakes was to tell children to cope and to be strong and independent. Too often we are expecting our children to do for themselves what we as parents should be doing for them. We need to teach instead of telling. We need to teach them all they need to know so that they can cope with the situations they find themselves in, and we need to teach them about their strength and power. Often victims of bullying believe themselves helpless and will endure the bullying, or try to handle it themselves in quite the wrong way, because they think that if they tell anyone they will be told not just that there is no help available from that person, but that they should be ashamed of looking for help at all.

In extreme cases, suicide may be chosen as the only way out of intolerable circumstances. Victims of bullying at boarding school often console themselves by thinking, 'If I can't stand it any more I have a way out, I can jump in the lake.' Feeling that they can escape, that they have some choice, helps such people not to feel completely trapped and at the mercy of the bullies. They feel they still have some independence, some control over their own fate.

Some victims also run away from home without any idea of how to manage except by joining the homeless living on the streets. These facts, plus similar facts about adults, plus statistics on suicides (for example, over 400 suicides per year in the Republic of Ireland), accidents, the homeless and the abused, demonstrate the need for more education on safety, coping skills, choices and interdependence.

It does not make sense to teach children, 'Don't get involved. Stand on your own two feet. Fight your own corner.' But what should we teach them instead?

Instead of 'Don't get involved', possibly, 'Don't make matters worse'. Under that you can give safety and first aid training so that their skills increase year by year (*see* Help). Tell them that if they can't help themselves, they *must* ask someone else for help.

It is tragic that, as disclosed by teachers, the ISPCC, the Rape Crisis Centre and others, matters are still not being set right for some children who are telling. Also, sadly, there are still children not telling but accepting abuse as their lot in life. It is important to stress that saying No and telling are the right things to do, and that, eventually, they do work for most people who persevere.

You can tell a small child that, just as it is better for a baby to cry when it really needs something, so it is better for a small child to come and tell if anything is the matter. You can continue to give that message as the child grows older, so they always confide in you, talk things over, plan what to do and let you know whether it worked out well or not. That way you can nip bullying in the bud, because you'll be told about it in the early stages and will be able to check whether it stops or not.

Therefore, instead of 'Stand on your own two feet and fight your own corner,' I suggest we teach, *'You are not helpless. There is help available. Use it.'*

Justice

JUSTICE may be defined as the rendering of what is due or merited. Equity and fairness are synonyms for justice.

By definition, bullying, with its connotations of deceit, trickery, betrayal, hypocrisy, misrepresentation, isolation, blackmail and more, is injustice. But it can be stopped by justice.

To see justice done we need to know who is guilty. Once it is established exactly where the guilt lies, then, as far as that matter is concerned, everyone else is innocent.

When dealing with the person who is guilty of bullying or abuse, we should take account of everything that contributed to their decision to act as they did. This is necessary, so that justice can be done to them and so that the consequences to that person are fair.

What a person does is that person's responsibility. If someone else gives the order for the thing to be done, they are more guilty of the offence than the underling who carries it out. If someone damages the guilty person's character and personality by some form of abuse, they are guilty of that abuse and should bear the blame for it; but they are not responsible for the specific actions taken by the person abused.

It is not justice if the consequence of an action bears no relation to that action; it is not justice if the guilty party gets off scot free; and nor is it justice if the consequence is a penalty that is too severe or too light.

What makes matters worse?

Bullying and injustice affecting the child, anything that makes their family unhappy, a lot of vandalism, theft and bully-gangs in the neighbourhood, bullying and injustice at school and at the local church or community centre, doom and gloom in the news and unwholesome TV programmes, videos and video games makes matters worse.

Sometimes a child says, 'It's not fair. That's not fair. There's no justice in that,' and a grown-up says, 'Welcome to the real world. Life's not fair. You have to put up with it and learn to work the system.' The only thing worse than giving children such a black outlook is to paint too rosy a picture. If you pretend that everyone is good, honest and fair and that justice is always done, then your child will be shattered when he/she discovers you lied. This will be even worse if you maintain the fiction after your child knows that you know about grave injustices being done to him/her by bullying or other abuse.

What actually helps?
It is a great help if, within the family, every effort is made to be loving, honest, fair and kind. It also helps if the child learns good behaviour, basic necessary skills and assertiveness before going to school. It helps a lot if you choose a school which has a good code of discipline and ethics, a code which includes an anti-bullying policy. It helps even more if the teachers try their best to be fair and spend a lot of time helping the children to learn to value themselves and others, and to care about courtesy, consideration, respect, honour, truth and justice. (*See* **Classroom Management**.) This not only gives children a happy childhood, but good habits for life and friends with high ideals. Because they have experienced a just regime, children will know what is involved in achieving justice and a good atmosphere, so they have some chance of establishing this where they work and live and, in time, within their own family.

The influence of a teacher is very great. You sometimes find, out of twelve classes in a school, only one or two where every child has the guts to 'own up' to their peccadillos. It is sad where children in a class care nothing for justice, so that some claim the right to silence, some falsely claim innocence, some make false accusations, some worry only about proving their own innocence but won't help bring the whole truth out into the open. (*See* **Independence**.)

Children will grow to understand that nobody is perfect, and that justice and self-respect require us to take responsibility for our actions and, when appropriate, to say, 'Sorry,' and to make amends.

Letters

Sample complaints letter to a School Board of Management (BOM). *The letter should be addressed to the Chairperson of the BOM, or to the Parents' Representative of the BOM; both names are obtainable from the school secretary or principal.*

Dear

I wish to draw your attention to certain matters which are causing a great deal of concern to us as parents of children at [X] School.

Firstly some children have been slapped by [name of teacher] in the classroom/ corridor/schoolyard. We know that the Department of Education does not permit teachers to use corporal punishment. We trust that the BOM will inform [teacher's name] that the complaint has been made, and will ensure that in future corporal punishment is not inflicted on any child at this school.

Secondly, we are aware that Department of Education regulations do not allow teachers to make derogatory, humiliating statements to or about the pupils in the school. [Teacher's name] said, 'You are thick, you are stupid', to [child's name] in class recently [dates if possible].

Thirdly, discrimination or harassment because of race, ethnic origin, family background et cetera will soon be illegal in the workplace and in places providing services including, education. When [child's name] came to school without her [for example] uniform, the teacher in question said to her, 'It's no wonder given the family you come from.'

Fourthly, we feel that all the children in remedial class should be assessed and their parents given information as to what help they need, for example whether it is with reading, writing, spelling, sums, comprehension, behaviour, artwork, co-ordination, peer relationships *et cetera*. We trust you will arrange this, and appreciate it will take time.

Fifthly, we would like more anti-bullying activities for the children at school.

Finally, we are sure you agree that the sooner problems are dealt with the better, and that it is in all our interests to have good parent-teacher communication and cooperation. Given the importance of these matters, we trust that within a few days we will have your reply informing us of the course of action decided on by the BOM.

Although we are unable to attend daytime meetings as we work during the day, we are available at any other time and are always ready to play our part as partners in our children's education. We believe that X School is a good school, and that the BOM will feel, as we do, that dealing satisfactorily with any complaints demonstrates the high standards expected of a good school.

Yours sincerely...

Also finish with the names of the children, their class and their year teacher.

You may also want to name any older children who might have attended the same school; give for each child the year s/he completed school, and say what school, if any, they are at now.

Sample Letter from CaB to researcher

Dear

In your letter of [date] you say you are a student at X, studying [subject].

Bullying permeates society at all levels and is evident in all areas, so it is right that projects on bullying feature on many courses (though as yet still quite unusual). In the Republic of Ireland all schools have the *Department of*

Education Guidelines on Countering Bullying Behaviour.
Most libraries have books on bullying. All schools in the UK
have received many packs and booklets on bullying, the
most recent being the 120-page-plus book produced by the
Sheffield researchers, Smith *et al.* If your library has very
little on bullying, you could approach the nearest secondary
school for material in print. While you are there, you could
ask for permission to have a questionnaire given to one or
two classes to fill out, anonymously. Devise your own questions to obtain answers giving information useful and
appropriate to your course – i.e., include questions on bullying
and perhaps on cooperation, competition, sport, leisure and
recreation, work, holidays, recent purchases, favourite
books, films, videos and TV programmes.

If you can't get the cooperation of a school, ask family
and friends to help get at least twelve people to fill in the
questionnaire. The Olweus questionnaire, which is copyright, has questions about friends; being bullied; liking
break-time; where bullying happens; if bullies are the same
age as the victim; frequency of bullying; teacher's input –
that is, prevention, intervention, course of action taken;
whether people tell/stop the bullying/join in etc.; the number
of people known to be bullied/bullies; bullies who are not
fellow pupils; parents' attitude to bullying.

I hope this is sufficient to help you to devise your own set
of questions.

It is essential that your questionnaire states explicitly
what counts as bullying; if you do not want a wide definition, then I think you should add separate questions on abuse
in general, isolated incidents of violence, fights, quarrels and
lies. Some definitions of bullying are indeed very wide. CaB
includes all abuse within its definition. One English school
includes all unkind words and actions (something which can
cause problems, because discipline and truth often hurt as
well as helping, and anything that hurts can be called
unkind. Abuse, on the other hand, is always wrong by definition – as is injustice).

I wish you well with your project.

Letter to a parent of an ex-victim of bullying

Dear

Please read all these notes with your son. Also, please ask the psychologist to go over them with your son at the next meeting. Keep your son away from school until you've spoken to the principal of the co-ed school; say you've been in touch with me and that your son and all his family are working through the notes I've sent you. Say that I said the school staff are responsible for the safety and welfare of the pupils in their care. Say that other schools are implementing Whole School anti-bullying programmes, so it is high time they did too. Say you want your son's safety guaranteed for the remaining four weeks of term, especially for the summer exams, and that you will be sending your son to the all-boys school from September.

But first go to see the principal of the all-boys school so you can say the above. Telephone for an appointment, and when you see him explain that the co-ed school has a serious bullying problem and that there is a great use of bad language such as calling his school 'the school for faggots'. Your son cannot concentrate in such an atmosphere, which is especially wasteful as he is intelligent and talented. Explain that your son is learning strategies to avoid being picked on, and how to deal with any bullying situation. Have the notes with you. Assure him that your son will be sensible, quiet and hard-working.

Best wishes.

Letter to an ex-victim of bullying

Dear

Injustice makes most people very angry. You have been unfairly treated by your schoolmates and by your school-teachers. Victims of bullying should be helped by their parents, relations, friends, neighbours, schoolteachers, community leaders, etc., etc. If this help is not forthcoming or is insufficient, the victim feels angry, helpless (literally), disappointed, disillusioned, even hopeless and back to angry; she or he is caught in a circle of negative emotions. This is not your fault – it is basically the bullies' fault. At this stage they've got what they want – that is, the power to make you miserable. It is perverted, sick, wicked and sadistic to take pleasure in causing pain. The victim of bullying, however unhappy she or he may be, has not sunk as low as that. The victim is still clear about what is good, bad, right, wrong, enjoyable, disgusting, healthy, sick, sensible, stupid.

Bullies tend to choose to do bad, wrong, disgusting, sick and stupid things like stealing, cheating, telling lies, bullying, abusing drugs and alcohol, joy-riding etc. The bullies' parents and teachers are failing in their duty to them if they do not reform/rehabilitate them, and teach them to conform to proper standards and to enjoy normal behaviour.

Everyone needs to be clear in their own heads about their priorities, their aims and goals and values. The first step to achieving what you want is to complete an Aspirations Chart, and then find out how to achieve all the items listed. Your position is a little like that of someone who has been kidnapped and abandoned on a desert island. Your predicament is not your fault and you have a right to be angry; but getting back to a normal life is going to be difficult and will take determination and hard work. Clearly, if you were on a desert island you would have to exert yourself just to survive. If you were hurt in an accident that wasn't your fault, you would also have to exert yourself to get fit and healthy again.

Being angry is normal, but what is important is working, with help, to get your life the way you want it. That takes real courage and real strength of character, and really deserves respect.

Here is one sample Aspirations Chart – copy the headings and under each write as much as you think of.

Aspirations Chart

A. *For myself*

A1. *Good relationship with God* (How: by prayer and ...)

A2. *Good relationship with parents* (How: communication, honest talk, appreciation and discussion. Learn to say what I feel bad about without feeling hate or anger, and without casting blame or guilt. Assume problems can be solved by talking them through, finding solutions and carrying these out. Also ...)

A3. *Possible career choices*

A4. *Necessary exam qualifications*

A5. *A social life, friends* (How: join clubs, sports or hobbies/clubs ...)

A6. *Safety, no bullying* (How: learn words and techniques.

B. *For my parents*

Solve my problems with their help, so improving atmosphere at home and relieving them of stress and anxiety. Also taking on a chore or two to give them time for family recreation like hill walking and picnics etc.

C. *For my brothers/sisters*

Help them achieve their goals. Share joy and laughter.

D. *For my friends*

Enjoy their company doing things that we all enjoy. Show interest in what they care about. Confide a little in them. Don't hog the conversation. Don't look bored when they talk. Everyone shares some interests, e.g. food, TV, the weather. List these interests:

Lies/Deceit in Bullying

'Truth is the first casualty of War. All they discover (when they visit Osijik in Croatia) is that no one can be trusted, no one is at ease and no one tells the truth.' *Radio Times*, 25 July 1994.

Here is the key to understanding the problem of bullying. In every bullying situation you will find lies and deceit. Lies are part and parcel of bullying. Lies perpetuate bullying. While the abuse of power is at the heart of bullying behaviour, deceit fills the head. In all your attempts to eliminate and prevent bullying, you will be hindered most by lies and deceit.

Nine kinds of lie occur in bullying:

- 'The victim is to blame.'
- 'It was fun and games, not bullying.'
- 'It was an accident, fight or isolated incident, not bullying.'
- 'The choice is between having bullies as friends or having no friends at all, and the former is better.' A double lie.
- 'Threats such as 'I'll kill you' and 'I'll burn your house down' are usually lies.
- 'Nobody will believe you.' This is a powerful combination of *threat* and *denial*.
- 'It didn't happen; it's not true.' Denial like this may be culpable ignorance rather than a lie.
- Casting doubt in order to weaken the victim's self-confidence or to weaken other people's confidence in the victim.
- Misinformation. This includes hypocrisy, obstruction, withholding of information, truth-telling in a manner designed to provoke disbelief, taking credit for another's work, and rubbishing another's performance. Also obfuscation – the work of the spin doctor.

Insidious lies such as these undermine trust. Bullying can be eliminated only if people value truth, justice and desire happiness for themselves and others. Let us now look in more detail at each lie in turn.

Bullying is wrong, unjustifiable and undeserved, but:

'The victim brought it on herself.'

This has proved to be a very successful lie. When seeking an explanation for bullying, most people look for something in the victim's personality and behaviour before, during and after each bullying incident – explanations can include: 'She's different, and the bully homes in on that'; 'He's very fat and that makes him a target'; 'She's picked on because she doesn't dress like the others'; 'She was very irritating'; 'He didn't stand up for himself'; 'She's a brainbox'; 'He's very well-mannered.'

Victims hear this kind of explanation from all sides and generally come to believe that some attribute of their own is to blame. If that attribute is something they can change, they will do it if possible; if they can't change it they may become desperate. In that frame of mind, a victim can believe that their skin colour, accent, exam marks or whatever is the actual *cause* of the bullying. Even books on bullying sometimes suggest that difference triggers the bullying. *This is not true.* Mixed messages – on one hand, 'You do not deserve this. You have a right to be safe. Tell', and on the other, 'You are bringing this on yourself by being there, wearing that, feeling that, saying that' – give no hope to the victim.

Scapegoating is another manifestation of this lie. Sadly, in Ireland as elsewhere, there have been cases where a family scapegoat died from ill-treatment and neglect. Scapegoating also happens in the workplace. It is a form of bullying and abuse, and it places the blame unfairly on the victim.

'It wasn't bullying – it was only a game. We were only messing.'

Again this lie is a very successful one, because the victim, if he doesn't report the incident as bullying, will often go along with the bully's story for fear of making matters worse, for shame at being seen to be a victim, or for shame at seeming disloyal.

When the victim does say that the incident was a bullying one, she may be accused of being the real bully, pretending to enjoy the fun till the authority figure turns up, then falsely turning on the erstwhile innocent playmates. This accusation can then be used as an excuse for the isolation and exclusion of the victim by an ever-wider group. Sometimes a victim who reports a bullying incident is accused of cowardice, pretence and disloyalty, and of getting the group into trouble. Again the incident can be falsely represented to peers to justify exclusion of the victim. In other words, the bully may also use the lie of misinformation to cast doubt on the victim's veracity.

This is a problem which can stump many authority figures, as it makes it very difficult to establish who is telling the truth. However, teachers and parents can set limits, defining acceptable behaviour, and there are courses of action which can be followed if someone is hurt or there is conflict to be resolved.

If, as an authority figure, you do nothing about a bullying situation, it will be assumed that you condone it or that you are ineffectual.

'It was an accident, fight or isolated incident – not bullying.' This lie is frequently successful when the matter comes down to the victim's word against the bully's. Believing the bully is easier because it means that there is no need for an authority figure to take any action. The lie is compounded by the false accusation that the victim is lying.

It is vital that as an authority figure you do not accept false excuses and test to see if the behaviour of the parties and the evidence are consistent with the claim. If a hurt was not intended there will be sincere attempts to help; if a hurt is greater than intended there will be remorse; if a hurt is really an isolated incident there will be a convincing reason why it happened, and neither the bullies nor the victim will have been involved in similar incidents before. It helps if fighting is forbidden in the relevant code of conduct.

'It's a choice between having bullies as friends or having no friends at all, and the former is better.'

This group of lies is successful because friendship is of inestimable value; we need friends, we are safer with friends. Having a lot of friends is greatly admired and desired. So a bully-gang can lure victims into joining the gang, then trick them into giving the gang their things because 'friends share'. They can con the victims into believing that what the gang does is fun or good (conformity being all-important here), and can mislead them into keeping bad secrets because 'friends are loyal'. The illusion of group protection makes victims believe that mistreatment by gang members is a sign of affection, while discipline by parents or teachers is oppressive cruelty. In other words, bad is good and good is bad – the ultimate lie.

Note all the forms of deception in the above passage – *pretence*, *luring*, *tricking*, *conning*, *misleading*, *illusion* – and the bully-speak inversions: mistreatment = affection, discipline = cruelty, good = bad, bad = good.

These lies are reinforced by adult behaviour. Why? We value friendship, we desire it for ourselves and for our children, and we admire popular people. We use our children's natural desire for friends to make them heed our instructions, saying, 'You won't have any friends if you are selfish, greedy, sulky, lazy, stupid, bad-tempered etc., etc., etc.' And because we want them to be popular for their sakes and for our own pride, we push them out to make friends, saying, 'Don't be shy. Make friends. You've got to learn to mix.'

Where there is a strong tradition of not 'telling tales', parents tell their children, 'Sort it out yourself. Stand up for yourself. Answer back. Hit back. Don't whinge. Don't be a crybaby. Don't be silly.' This gives a huge amount of power to children, and power corrupts. The mother of a nine-year-old girl bully told me, 'Everyone wanted to play with my daughter. She couldn't handle so much power. It went to her head. She didn't realise the damage it caused a child if she said, ''No, you can't play with me any more.'' She couldn't know the other children would ostracise a child that she excluded; nor how that child would feel, nor the fear the others had lest they offend her and fall from favour.' It doesn't help an ostracised child in that situation to be told to go out and play, to join in and not sit by herself.

Things can be even tougher where the bully is motivated by jealousy, especially if he gets a hard time at home from bullying siblings and over-strict, over-critical parents, and has a lot of hurt to pass on.

'If you can't beat 'em, join 'em' is terrible advice, born of low self-esteem. 'I'm not lowering my standards,' said one teenage acquaintance with the courage of her convictions. She gained more respect, lost nothing of value and remained popular.

When a bully claims to be your best friend, she will almost always break up your real friendships. Lies are told to the victim and about the victim, to damage relationships and self-image and to put victims in the wrong – and the sort of lies consisting of real remarks quoted out of context can be particularly cruel.

It can be very sad when friends grow apart and spend less time together, but there need not be enmity or bullying. Sometimes, however, an erstwhile best friend becomes increasingly jealous, malicious, and bitter and wants to hurt and bully the former friend. These negative emotions and bad behaviour can in turn lead to rebellion against goody-goody standards and to worse mischief, ranging from substance abuse to vandalism, underage drinking to joy-riding. One taunt used to the former best friend is that she is a baby, out of it, whereas the bully and the bully's in-crowd have lots of grown-up, glamorous, exciting fun. This is a very effective form of bullying, especially among teenagers. The members of the bully's in-crowd bully each other in the usual ways, including all the kinds of lie.

A favourite form of bullying among so-called friends is 'I won't be your friend any more unless you do what I say.'

This is also a lie, as a real friend does not abuse her power that way. The threat itself may be genuine or a bluff. If threat is a bluff, it is yet another lie – a threat.

Threats
In this chapter, by definition threats such as 'I'll kill you' are bluff and bluster, but it is not easy to distinguish bluffs from real threats, except with hindsight and experience. If in doubt, be careful. Bullies often say, 'You'd better do what I say or else.' Sometimes they spell out what they mean by 'else'. Sometimes they find it more effective, and much safer, to leave the consequence to the victim's imagination.

As always, it is best to be sensible, be assertive. Tell. Get help and support. Always try to take the heat out of a bullying situation. Don't issue challenges. Don't be passive or submissive either, though it can work to say, 'Sure, okay,' as the bully does not know whether that means you will do what he/she has demanded or not. Don't, of course.

'No one will believe you.'
This combination of threat and denial is well known and effective. Again, the advice of Stay Safe is for the victim to tell and keep telling until someone believes and helps him. Also, the victim should try some means of self-help – for example, some schoolchildren avoid being bullied by going to the library together rather than walking alone in the school grounds.

The more people who are told about bullying, the more the options for safety and protection that are open to the victim.

Denial
Not all denial is harmful or negative – 'It's no bother', 'Oh, the baby was no trouble'. Denial as both a lie and a type of bullying, however, takes many forms. One form is where the bully claims the victim's version of the truth is not true. 'They did that.' 'No, we didn't.'

Another form of denial which involves bullying as an abuse of power, causing harm and distress to the victim, is where someone refuses to admit that they have a problem which needs to be addressed. Instead of tackling the problem, they deny it, and someone suffers as a result. Out of fear and weakness and vanity the bullies or their parents/families may say things like:

'My child has perfect sight/hearing and does not need an eye/ear test.'

'My child would never bully anyone. Your accusation is false.'

'There is no bullying in this school.'

'There is no such illness as ME.'

'You are not ill' (instead of 'We have not yet identified what is wrong with you').

'I am not an alcoholic. You are a nag.'

'Your child is not dyslexic. Your child is stupid, lazy and inattentive.'

'Bullying does not cause a victim to underachieve.'

'Bullying does not cause eczema, asthma, insomnia, panic attacks.'

'They did not contribute to the success of this project – it was all my work.'

'You have been advised incorrectly; it's not my department.'

'I did not say that. I would not say that. You misheard.'

'Lies are not a form of bullying.'

'Bullying behaviour is never learnt at school – it comes from the home.'

'What guidelines? We never got any guidelines sent to our school.'

If you are aware of these common forms of denial, you can reply appropriately instead of being taken in by them.

Casting doubt.
Bullies cast doubt in order to weaken the victim's self-confidence, and to weaken the confidence of others in the victim. Victims of workplace bullying have said, 'I began to wonder if I was imagining the whole thing, making mountains out of

molehills, losing my grip on reality, having a mental break down.' Here are some stories to illustrate this subtle form of bullying:

'Are you sure it was not just a social telephone call?' This was said by a headmaster to a schoolgirl, Anne, and her parents when they reported that a group of bullies, who had been unkind to Anne for months, had further upset Anne by a phone call the previous weekend. The bullies had said that they were phoning to cheer Anne up because she was prob- ably alone and lonely, whereas they had had a lovely time at a slumber party. 'Aren't we good to think of you?' they had asked, laughing and tittering.

'They did not mean to exclude you – they just became engrossed in a private conversation.' This was said by a youth-club leader to a club member, John. John had reported that he and four others were sitting chatting in a group when Pete came up and got between John and the others, who all put their heads together to talk. John could not hear or join in; he was physically excluded by the new closed-circle position of the others, and ignored when he spoke up.

'They probably forgot they had promised you that.' Parents say this when their child rages that his/her class- mates or other acquaintances have broken a promise such as 'We'll phone to let you know where we're meeting up' or 'We'll pick you up at the café at six o'clock.' Sometimes it is forgetfulness or unforeseen circumstance that causes the promise to be broken, but sometimes it is bullying.

'When you've calmed down it won't seem so bad.' This suggests that the victim is over-reacting, and can badly shake her self-confidence, particularly if she is not over-reacting.

'Of course, you are still very angry, however ...' This suggests that the victim has no good reason to be so angry. It is right to be angry at cruelty and injustice to yourself or others, especially where children have been hurt.

'Forgive and forget and let it all blow over.' This is sometimes said even when the same abominable things will happen over and over again unless something decisive is done.

'You are focusing on this but the real problem is some-thing else.' This is something that is often said in a doctor's surgery. The patient complains about specific pains in the shoulder, the intestines or the foot, and the doctor suggests it is all old age or the menopause or family worries.

'Her memory is going, poor dear, and she has a grudge ...' This is typical of a workplace situation where colleagues use a couple of minor memory lapses, plus the fact that she was at some stage passed over for promotion, to bully a fellow worker. The stress is likely to cause the victim to make more mistakes, turning the taunt into a self-fulfilling prophecy.

'And you believed that?!' This says that the victim is a gullible fool, when the message should be, 'They are shocking liars.'

'She is hysterical. She is emotionally disturbed. She needs a psychiatrist.' This is too often said to victims of bullying, even those who have been physically injured.

Misinformation
Under this category comes a rag-bag of forms of misinfor-mation such as hypocrisy, obfuscation, changing rules, shifting goalposts, insincere apologies, promises made to be broken, and the withholding of information, especially of information regarding the non-implementation of promised action and as a delaying tactic so one runs out of time and energy before gaining the information sought. The expressed hope in this instance is that the problem will have 'resolved itself', although the real risk is that it will become serious and intractable.

Bullies like using misinformation because it is easy, causes a lot of harm and, because it looks like ignorance, incompe-tence or error, can be difficult to identify as bullying. Here are some examples of this type of lie:

A teacher thanks a parent for bringing a problem to her attention and promises, 'I'll deal with it and keep you informed.' Weeks later the parent says to the teacher, 'The bullying is still going on. What exactly did you do about it?' The teacher says, 'Oh, I spoke to the children your child said were bullying. They were surprised your child was upset, a they are all friends', or 'I'm so sorry for you and your child, but there is nothing I can do to stop the bullying because I've had no training in it', or 'I told your child to toughen up and look more confident.' The parent feels let down because the promised feedback has not materialised. A promise of feedback generally means nothing unless a date, time and place have been fixed for it, and even then this date can be postponed or cancelled.

For instance, at work you may turn up for a meeting to find the room empty. Although you weren't informed that the meeting was cancelled, rumours may begin to fly about your competence.

Delaying tactics on the phone include, 'The person you want is busy, will you hold or shall I take your number and have them call you back?' Some call back, many do not. You can be asked to 'put it in writing', after which you receive a 'holding' letter and nothing further. If a matter is important to you, don't be too patient and don't be too trusting. Also, find out if there are resources or procedures that would assist you.

These nine lies described above, as well as being forms of bullying in themselves, undermine efforts to counter bullying. In particular, the 'Cool Schools' Peer Mediation for Conflict Resolution (*see* **Mediation**) cannot work unless the participants are honest.

Remember the seven-year-old who was told not to be a telltale shortly after her class had completed the Stay Safe lessons in which they'd been taught to 'Say no. Get away. Tell someone you can trust'. When her parents asked her what she had learned in school today, her answer was: 'I know now that teachers are liars and hypocrites.'

Logic

'Questioning the validity of Reason is the thought that destroys thought.' G. K. Chesterton.

FEW people think logically. However, most of us tell each other to be reasonable, especially when the subject of bullying arises.

Those of us who think logically cannot believe self-contradictory statements, and reject faulty reasoning: for example 'That doesn't follow.' We can, however, despite our clear thinking, make false statements because we are mistaken, are misinformed or because we choose to lie.

Because most of us think rationally (most of the time!), it is not so good to feel stymied and nonplussed by irrational people. Bullies can cut the ground from under us by denying the facts, reasoned arguments and evidence that give us support. This is an effective bullying technique, especially if the victim is unprepared for it.

The ability to think logically does not carry with it a guarantee of morality. It is just a useful tool which can be used to good or ill purpose. We don't expect intelligent, educated people to deny facts and valid argument, or to make replies that totally miss the point, and at first it throws us when this happens. Bullies may think clearly but seem not to, because they are devious and feel safer when shrouded in veils of secrecy and obfuscation. Bullies love half-truths and false rumours. Bullies know that strong emotions can fog the brain, and know how to use that fact for their own power and advantage. Bullies love to feel superior and to see their victims nonplussed. However, what you don't value, you lose. Eventually even the cleverest bullies are no longer able to think clearly and are unable to avoid exposure as objects of contempt. Many public figures who behave in a bullying manner may be ridiculed very effectively and entertainingly by satirists such as Rory Bremner.

The subject of smacking children is one that prompts a great deal of argument, much of it unreasonable. For instance, the illogical proposition that 'All X are Y means all Y are X' can be used to argue that 'all violent abusers are people who were slapped as children, therefore all people who were slapped as children are violent abusers.' It is plainly untrue that slapping children leads to violence. Similarly, it is stated that slapping, or any other punishments, promote the belief that 'Might is right' whereas what good authority figures are trying to do is show that 'Right has might'. Equally, 'either A or not-A' usually holds. Either A: children should have total freedom to do whatever they choose; or Not-A: their freedom must be limited. If people wish to argue against Not-A in the above, they must defend A which so far they have not dared to do.

A further illogical tenet is that 'only those in authority can be guilty of abuse of power'. But everyone has the power to hurt and destroy. Time and again we find people in charge of a family home, school, prison or a refugee camp are not allowed to use even a modicum of force to keep order, while those they are in charge of can commit all sorts of violence against each other. To a logical person that is insanity. To a fair person it is injustice. To the people involved it is The Rules.

Fashionable opinions, supported by specious arguments, can contend with common sense, supported by logic, and this hinders those working for peace and justice.

ME
(Myalgic Encephalomyelitis)

ME is a chronic fatigue syndrome (CFS) caused by viral infection(s) plus other stressors such as overwork, extremes of heat or cold, and bereavement. People with ME have abnormalities in blood, muscle and brain cells, and in the blood-flow to the brain, but this does not mean there is an easy diagnostic test for ME.

To determine whether you have ME, you should go to the doctor and arrange to have tests to check whether your symptoms are in fact caused by some other disorder such as an ovarian cyst, lupus, intestinal parasites, candida, low blood sugar, low thyroid activity, diabetes etc.

It is worthwhile doing the Romberg test, as that will demonstrate physical balance impairment: in dim light (so that you can't balance by focusing on light through the eyelids), eyes closed, arms by sides, without shoes, feet together, stand still for three minutes if you can. You should have somebody with you and cushions round you in case you fall. Those who are very tired or convalescing after an illness will start to sway after about thirty seconds (although if you are fairly healthy you will be able to correct this easily). The Romberg test is also a handy quick check on robust fitness! If there is a serious balance problem a neurologist may be able to help you to better health.

The diagnosis of ME is made by excluding other illnesses and checking the ME symptoms list. Fatigue plus three or more other symptoms suggests that ME is likely. If you have ME, you must rest a lot, and you must stop any activity before you feel tired, because if you get tired you are likely to relapse and may be ill and exhausted for a very long time, anything from two days to two years.

The first symptom, then, is *fatigue*, usually made worse

by physical exercise. Sometimes the ill effects of exercise are not apparent until a day or two after you have over-exerted yourself, whereas the normal reaction is to feel tired after exercise but to feel recovered the next day. With ME, the fatigue may be so great that you may even feel ill and exhausted just trying to walk across the room.

Other symptoms of ME include *difficulty enunciating words clearly*, *saying the wrong words* especially names, *difficulty finding the word you want*, *memory lapses*, especially short-term memory failure, *difficulty in paying attention or concentrating*, feeling *irritable, anxious or depressed*, when tired feeling *weepy and shaky, nightmares, difficulty sleeping, headaches* especially pressure headaches, *eye problems* such as blurring and difficulty focusing and extreme sensitivity to light, extreme *sensitivity to noise, tinnitus*, i.e. noises in the ears like buzzing, droning or ringing, *numbness* and *pins and needles, difficulty with balance*, e.g. bumping into things, stumbling and tottering, *dropping things*, things *taste, smell, sound, feel and look different from usual, muscle spasms* – hard cramps, muscle weakness, soft as a sponge, *muscle pain, joint pain, bone pain, lymph nodes pain, abdominal pain, low-grade fevers, flushes, sweats, intolerance of heat or cold*; *bowel, bladder and menstrual problems*; *frequent recurrent 'flu-like illnesses and tummy bugs, allergies*, especially new food allergies with reactions like falling asleep and then feeling very sick for a day or two, or feeling as if a jelly-fish had stung you inside, or itches and rashes or feeling 'spaced out'; *swelling and weight gain, heart palpitations* – like a butterfly in the chest, *pressure on the chest*, especially on waking up, *poor circulation* to hands and feet, *cold ears, blackouts*.

Bullying does not cause ME; however, ME is exacerbated by stress, and bullying problems are stressful. Those who have ME are especially vulnerable to various kinds of bullying as, indeed, are all those with any kind of illness or disability. In the case of ME there is still scepticism about whether it is a 'real illness' or a form of hypochondria or depression. In consequence, some people with ME suffer grave injustices from medical, social welfare and employment personnel, as well as a lack of understanding from most other people.

Most people who become ill with ME make a recovery to between 50 and 80 per cent of their former level of good health, and are able to return to work and to more normal pursuits. It is advisable for the return to work to be gradual – part-time at first if possible.

For further information, try the following:

Dr Anne Macintyre: *ME Post-Viral Fatigue Syndrome. How to Live with It.*
Michael Reed Gach: *Arthritis Relief at Your Fingertips.*
Tuula Tuormaa: *An Alternative to Psychiatry* (on allergies).

Irish Contacts
The Irish ME Support Group, PO Box 3075, Dublin 2; 17 Charlemont, Griffith Avenue, Dublin 9; 36 Stillorgan Grove, Blackrock, Co. Dublin (01) 288 4927; fax (01) 660 3081.
Irish ME Trust, 18 Upper Fitzwilliam Street, Dublin 2; PO Box 28838 Dublin 2 (01) 676 1413; (fax) 676 1534.

UK Contacts
ME Action, PO Box 1302, WELLS, Somerset BA5 2WE, England

Further details of ME contacts in Ireland, the UK and other countries can be obtained from any of the above and from the InterNet.

Mediation

FIGHTING, squabbling or bullying, whether in the home, the school or the workplace, must be stopped. But unless the causes of the conflict are tackled, the problem will arise again. If there is to be peace, the people in conflict must come to an agreement, whether by themselves or through a third party. For example, two children may be squabbling over which TV programme to watch. If they continue to squabble and keep changing channels, or if a parent sends them to their room for fighting, then neither will see the programme of their choice. Most kids will come to a mutually acceptable agreement by themselves or with the help of someone else, usually a parent, babysitter or friend.

To resolve conflict in a way that is as fair as possible, you need information and advice, skills in counselling and mediation, a support group and powerful helpers, common sense and common decency. This chapter is about mediation, how to go about it, and the sort of training that improves a mediator's skills.

Chairpersons of school boards of management have said they would welcome training in conflict-resolution skills to help them resolve the conflicts at board meetings. It seems obvious to me that everyone needs conflict-resolution skills, although the terminology itself is one that few of us would use. In fact, if you are teaching six-year-olds the peer-mediation method of conflict resolution it would be wiser not to give it a name but to say, 'Suppose you see a couple of your classmates fighting or squabbling, you could offer to help to sort it out.' They'll probably call themselves 'helpers' or 'sorter-outers' or 'the one in the middle', rather than 'the mediator' or 'the counsellor', and that's fine. They might like to say, 'I'll be the Sage', especially if older children play the acronyms game or fantasy games.

How to Arrange a Mediation Session

1. The mediator arranges the session with the people in conflict (the *disputants*). The mediator calms the disputants and explains or reminds them of the format for a mediation session, that is:
2. Each disputant tells his/her story – that is, what they think happened. No interruptions are allowed. After each disputant has spoken, the mediator summarises what was said and checks if that summary is an accurate assessment of the speaker's perspective.
3. The mediator asks how each person feels about the situation.
4. The mediator asks each if they wish to add anything about facts or feelings, each time summarising what was said as often as necessary.
5. The mediator asks each to suggest possible solutions.
6. The mediator helps disputants to find areas of agreement in the suggested solutions, and so to find a solution that suits both.
7. If necessary, the mediator points out the benefits of reaching a solution and the consequences of not agreeing on a solution.
8. The aim is to find a win/win solution that is fair and to everyone's advantage as compared to continued conflict.
9. The mediator promises confidentiality, except where a fact stated is of the sort which must be reported by law/by school rules.
10. The mediator writes the agreement forms which the disputants sign and copy.
11. The mediator arranges a check-back time, and suggests to the disputants what they are to do if there is a serious problem before that time.
12. The mediator writes a report form, and later a check-back form.

Example

Toby sees Jane and Pete hitting and shouting at each other in the schoolyard. Toby goes up to them and offers to mediate by saying, 'Hey, you two, can I help sort this out? You know fighting is not allowed in this school.' Jane and Pete realise that if they refuse this offer, they'll be reported for fighting and the school principal will impose a penalty, so they prefer to agree to mediation.

Toby says, 'Shall we sit down over there or would you rather go to the library for this session?' Pete says, 'Here's fine.' Jane says, 'I want to go to the library – it's quieter and more comfortable.' Toby says, 'Is it OK with you if we use the library, Pete?' Pete says, 'I suppose so.'

They go to the library and sit in a triangle with Toby between Pete and Jane. Toby has a pencil and notebook. Toby says, 'You know the ropes. Which of you wants to speak first?' Jane and Pete both say, 'I'll go first.' Toby says, 'My dad always jokes that if the path is dangerous, ladies first, so let Jane speak first.'

Jane: Pete's always annoying me.

Toby: You know the rules, Jane. First of all, just say what happened in the yard today.

Jane: I was trying my shoelaces and Pete came up and pulled my plait and said 'Plain Jane is a pain' and laughed and ran off, so I ran after him and pulled his hair 'cos he'd pulled mine, and I told him off for being rude to me.

Toby: So, Jane, you were tying your shoelaces, Pete pulled your hair and said 'Plain Jane is a pain', laughed and ran off. You ran after him, pulled his hair and told him off.

Jane: Yes.

Toby: Well, Pete, is that what happened?

Pete: Yes, I guess. But I only tipped her hair and she pulled mine really hard, and she always calls me Pete Smelly-Feet, so I made a rhyme about her too.

Toby: So, Pete, you say you just tipped Jane's hair and said the rhyme because she's been calling you Pete Smelly-Feet, and you say Jane pulled your hair very hard.

Pete: That's right.

Toby: Jane, how do you feel about this?

Jane: I hate Pete. I wish he'd leave this school.

Toby: How do you feel, Pete?

Pete: If anyone does anything to me, I pay them back; they don't need to think they can get away with it. I've as much right to be in this school as Jane has.

Toby: Is there anything else either of you wants to tell me about this situation?

Pete, Jane: No.

Toby: How long has it been going on?

Jane: Ever since Pete came into this school last year. The very first day he bumped into me in the corridor and I bumped him right back and said, 'Watch who you bump!' He said it was an accident and I said, 'I bet you don't accidentally bump into the teachers, so don't bump into me either, OK?'

Pete: Jane never gives a fellow the benefit of the doubt. She can never take a joke either. But she doesn't need to think she can hit me and jeer at me and expect me to just take it.

Toby: Jane, what do you think would solve the problem?

Jane: I already said – Pete leaving the school.

Toby: That's not really an option, Jane. Pete, what do you suggest?

Pete: We could ignore each other.

Jane: Yes. We could just behave as if the other person wasn't there.

Toby: Although you both say you agree to ignore each other, that's really not a good solution in my opinion. You're both in the same class, so it will be very difficult, 'cos you're in the same room for five hours a day. Also, the teachers here wouldn't approve. They're always on about 'a good class atmosphere'. You've both seen how retaliation just keeps the problem going on and on and getting worse. You're both unhappy with fighting and you'll be in trouble if you're caught fighting. The teachers won't approve if you completely ignore each other. Perhaps you could acknowledge each other politely in class if you need to, and you could avoid each other as much as possible?

Jane, Pete: Yes. OK.

Toby: Do you feel that is fair and that it will be an improvement?

Jane, Pete: Yes.

Toby: If you don't fight any more, we can keep this confidential. I need you to sign the agreement and copy it out for yourselves to keep.

[The form reads: *I agree to avoid or be polite to Jane/Pete. I understand that if we fight again we will be reported for fighting. I understand that if I hit or jeer at Jane/Pete I'll be reported for it. Date; signature.*]

Check-back time: one week later. The next check-back time would be in a fortnight, then a month. Meanwhile Toby gives a message to the relevant teacher, either directly or through the school principal, that the class would benefit from revision of 'valuing ourselves and others', especially the importance of not jeering at people or calling them nasty names.

Most sessions are not as antagonistic as the example above. The disputants apologise and offer to make up by inviting each other home or out for a treat, or they exchange small gifts or lend each other favourite books. They promise to welcome each other into schoolyard games, and to keep their promise, and so on. Even in the above case, after a few weeks when the wounds have begun to heal and no new ones are inflicted, Pete and Jane will have a chance to discover that each can be quite good company when they are not too busy squabbling. Six months later, they might very well say, 'We got off on the wrong foot but now, thank to Toby's mediation, we are good friends.'

Sample Mediation Agreement Forms

I agree to do the following:-_____
I understand the consequences of not keeping the
agreement:- _____
Date:- _____
Signature:- _____
Check-back time:- _____

Mediators Report Form for Confidential File

The form filled out by the mediator should include the following: mediator's name; time and date of the session; the disputants' names; short description of the conflict'; the agreement reached, as described on the agreement form; the check-back time.

Dispensing with a Mediator

In the above case, Toby could have told Jane and Pete to negotiate between themselves, as the fighting could not be allowed to continue.

Slogans

Slogans – for instance on posters and tee-shirts – are useful when introducing mediation to any group. Examples include:

- *Don't fight – go for mediation*
- *Don't get mad – get a mediator*
- *Be my mediator and I'll be yours.*

Note: if the group comes up with a better slogan, that's the one to plump for.

Training in Mediation

Mediation requires equality, and this means that everyone should be trained in mediation skills. In other words, if you are going to use mediation in your home, school, club or workplace, you should make sure everyone learns the process for a mediation session and the following skills.

Class Lessons or Workshops

Important points to follow when training in mediation include:

Active listening. This means paying attention to the person speaking, asking relevant questions in order to eliminate vagueness or possible misapprehensions; giving feedback to show that one has a grasp of both the facts and the feelings recounted by the speaker; being ready to adjust feedback until it matches what the speaker is saying. Often it is only when the mediator listens that the disputants hear each other's side of the story.

It's not a good idea to use phrases, such as 'I hear what you're saying' or 'So your safety is important to you', that make the speaker doubt your sanity or your good faith. Counterproductive phrases like this are widely used.

Don't talk about yourself, but use your own experience and knowledge to help you frame questions that may elicit answers that will shed light on the conflict or problem.

Don't give advice, but you can ask, 'Has anyone ever suggested such and such?' rather than leave the disputants without a possible solution which they have not thought of.

Rules are there to help not to hinder or to handicap. If you feel hamstrung by the rules, they have probably been misapplied or misunderstood. If in doubt, ask.

Affirmations and 'I' statements (these are essential, but most people are very bad at them, particularly when it comes to saying something positive about themselves). It is vital to give examples and practice sessions. One way to do this is to go round the group several times; each time each person says their name and a statement about the topic set, for example: 'I am Kate and I like coffee', 'I am John and I have a pet cat called Misha' or 'I am Mary and I play tennis'. Another is to split the group into pairs. Each pair has to find out six things about each other, and then each person introduces his or her pair partner to the rest of the group, giving the information in a friendly way.

Another is for everyone in a small group to say, 'I like Mary and one reason I like her is because she is good fun', or 'I like John and one reason I like him is because we enjoy the same sports' – and so on about each person in the group, including themselves.

Recognising responses to conflict such as denial, confrontation, dirty tricks, problem-solving, offers to do specific things which would improve matters.

Denial – 'I don't have a problem.' 'I did not.'

Confrontation – 'It's your fault.' 'You lied.' 'You provoked.' 'You looked.'

Dirty tricks – intimidation, blackmail, lies, red herrings et cetera.

Problem-solving – genuine attempts to establish good relationships and prevent aggression.

The role of the mediator – best done by demonstrations and role-play.

The mediation process – the twelve steps as described above.

Handling difficult situations where disputants are interrupting, going off the point, slagging, lying, not cooperating, not attempting to suggest solutions. All good ideas are welcome.

Simple ways to describe feelings such as: 'I feel X when you Y because Z' – 'I feel bad when you are sad because I love you.' Provide a vocabulary of words such as *angry, helpless, furious, wild, humiliated, deflated, frustrated, jealous, crazy, weeping, diminished, a nobody.*

Sample agreements, contracts, solutions based on experience. For example: 'I agree not to hit Jane. If I feel like hitting Jane I will say, "I feel like hitting you, Jane, because _____"'; 'I promise I will not make fun of Pete no matter how much I want to'; 'I agree to say if I don't like something.'

Practice at cooperative games, ice-breaking activities such as finding out facts like each person's favourite foods, everyday breakfasts, opinions on TV programmes et cetera; organising a pursuit or event, where consensus is important and everyone is involved; taking turns at being the leader. Everybody makes suggestions and contributes ideas, and someone co-ordinates.

Practice at giving praise and constructive criticism.

Practice at giving rewards and showing appreciation.

Practice at saying, 'No', 'Stop', 'Don't', 'Watch out', et cetera. A mediator must be able to stop disputants if they slag, interrupt, bring in irrelevant details.

Mediation Role-Play

This is a very valuable exercise, as everybody will play every part. There should be no shortage of ideas for story-lines in your group, as everyone has experience of conflict. Divide your class or group into smaller groups of four, each of whom will take one of the following parts: Disputant 1, Disputant 2, Mediator, Observer. The observer notes good ideas, and makes sure the others play their parts and follow the rules.

Conclusion

Mediation skills are well worth developing and using. Eighty per cent success rates have been claimed by several schools which have used these techniques to eliminate bullying and fighting. Since 1984, mediation has been a basic component of the syllabus in Californian schools. But although a very useful tool, mediation is not a cure-all, for it can be prevented from working by lies, lack of cooperation and lack of control.

Noise

NOISE can certainly be used as a form of harassment. However, the wider problems of noise are also relevant to a book on bullying abuse.

Noise that Impairs Hearing

Noise that impairs hearing counts as abuse. Like so many injuries it may be self-inflicted, or it may be inflicted by others on people who could avoid it but do not, because they want to enjoy a class, a concert, a dinner-dance or disco, or a sport where there are noisy engines. Noise abuse may be inflicted on those who cannot avoid the building work, the roadworks or noisy machinery next door. And it may be inflicted on employees by employers ignoring the relevant safety regulations. Workers can take noise problems to their staff Health and Safety representative. Legislation governing noise in the workplace is implemented and effective some of the time; however, if there is legislation protecting voluntary partygoers, few know of it.

Even where lots of information and advice regarding precautions to prevent damaged hearing are given to children from as early as age five, the kids usually choose to accept some hearing impairment as an inevitable cost of the lifestyle they wish to follow – but at least this is an informed choice. However, in spite of such education, few people complain about the sound being too loud at concerts or in restaurants. Perhaps health and life-skills education in schools could be expanded to include assertiveness training, and role-playing at making complaints.

Noise that Annoys

Noise that annoys, although not dangerously loud in decibels, can be intolerable, disturbing the mental equilibrium even of the calmest person. From the torture of the dripping tap to the aggravation of someone else's favourite music, from the hum of the computer's cooling fan to that of the vacuum-cleaner, from toot of flute to blare of radio, from shouts and calls to miaous and barks – in every home there is a range of noises that occasionally cause nerves to fray and patience to snap.

So, how much has all this got to do with bullying? Well, first, when patience snaps we tend to snarl or shout or slam off, which can be a little unfair to those around us. Sometimes everyone is very understanding and forgiving: 'Sorry, have you a headache? What can I do to help?' Sometimes the aggravation escalates with: 'Well, it's not my fault and you didn't have to shout', and soon you can have lots of people feeling like victims and acting like bullies. This can happen very easily even in a happy home, but it is much more likely to happen between neighbours. Most people want to get on well with their neighbours at first, and few set out to bully them with noise while relationships are friendly. But it is inevitable that some sounds from next door will be annoying, and if unfair complaints and accusations are made, the problem can become much worse very quickly, with every sound being interpreted as intentional aggravation and retaliation.

So what can be done? The main aims are as follows:

* to avoid ill feeling as far as possible;
* to restore good-neighbourliness after all parties feel aggrieved;
* to cope with an unregenerate bad neighbour.

The first step in *avoiding ill feeling* is to make contact and chat a little. Find out if your neighbours are hypersensitive to noise or if they suffer from insomnia, and mention if you are/do. If you intend doing a lot of DIY, or if you plan to have builders in, mention this and promise to give fair warning before any unusual or noisy work commences. Accept and agree that newborn babies cry at night, and that healthy young children make a bit of clatter and can have carrying voices. Also accept that household appliances and lawn-mowers make a certain amount of noise. We all have the right to use these appliances, and so we must all find our own ways of coping with such noise if it bothers us. Some people can sleep peacefully in spite of thunderstorms and masonry drills, but few remain undisturbed by day or night, no matter what.

Don't use noisy power-tools at three o'clock in the morning. In court this would be judged a nuisance, and you would be ordered to restrict such use to normal daytime hours. If you are going to have a noisy party, perhaps invite your neighbours or at least apologise in advance and give some idea of how late the party will go on for. Don't have very frequent noisy parties if they disturb your neighbours – it is illegal anyway.

If your neighbour asks whether their noise did disturb you, be honest: if it did, say so but also, perhaps, say that one can put up with a little inconvenience once in a while for friends and neighbours. If you are bothered by avoidable noise from next door, choose a time when you are calm to tell your neighbours, and try to have a practical suggestion to the problem. Changing the time of day when something is done can solve some problems, changing the room used for practising music or for using power tools might work. If a prearranged time for noisy activity is arranged, you can plan to take your walk or do your shopping then. Most noise can be masked if you put on the television or some music, or do the vacuuming yourself. A couple of tapes specially record-ed to promote rest and relaxation and to relieve stress can be kept handy for when you need to sleep or rest. Earplugs and headphones suit some people and some circumstances – but not if you need to be able to hear the baby or the telephone.

If you know you are on edge and tense for other reasons, don't blame the noisy neighbour, even if the noise is the last straw. Try to ease the noise problem by the above sug-gestions and try to get help for all the other stress-inducing problems as well, using any available resource.

To restore good atmosphere after a falling-out over noise, it is a good idea, when you feel calmer, to go and talk things over in the hope that you and your neighbour can both agree to apologise and forgive each other. Have as full a discussion as possible of what the problems are, and what, if anything, can be done to improve things. Not everyone can be open, but it is well worth trying. Others may prefer to resume normal relations as if nothing had happened, and gradually try improving things by the suggestions discussed above. Sometimes a mutual friend or helpful neighbour can be asked to act as mediator to resolve the conflict. (*See* **Mediation**.) In some cases, the community garda/police officer is very skilful at restoring acceptable behaviour, especially if one party was really very much at fault and totally unrepentant until the garda's visit. A letter from your solicitor may achieve the desired result. If there is a landlord, he will explain to an offending tenant the rules regarding nuisance, including noise.

Where someone is an *unregenerate noisy bad neighbour* and you've tried everything, including legal action and court injunctions, all that remains is to find ways of avoiding the disturbance by using headphones, playing music, going out a lot, or moving house. It is worthwhile considering whether your choice is based on something more sensible than stubbornness. If you can not improve matters where you are, it is victim-speak to say, 'I'm not giving in. Why should I be the one to move?' If things are intolerable, whether at home, at work or at school, and if there is no prospect of a change for the better, at least consider moving somewhere else, especially if that is the advice from counsellors and friends.

When we reject what in our hearts we know to be good advice, we put a stress on ourselves that aggravates ill-health. Be honest with yourself, if only for the sake of your immune system.

Parents of a
Bullied Schoolchild

PARENTS of a bullied schoolchild can do a lot to prevent the situation recurring or becoming worse. Try the following suggestions:

1. Read books on bullying and parenting.
2. Attend courses on parenting, assertiveness and self-defence.
3. Join parents' groups such as the school parents' assoc., local residents' assoc., neighbourhood watch, NAPS (National Assoc. for Parent Support), NPCs et cetera.
4. Join or form a local community anti-bullying group.
5. Learn and teach your children safety Dos and Don'ts about first aid, electricity, fire, water, gas, traffic and bullying.
6. Tell your school principal about any bullying in your area, and ask for the written school plan, policy statement, code of conduct or code of discipline, the school safety statement and the September 1993 *Guidelines on Countering Bullying Behaviour in Schools* (for Ireland).
7. Ask your primary school for the INTO booklets *Tips for Parents* and *Discipline in the Primary School* (for Ireland).
8. Ask the school principal or board of management for Stay Safe to be taught throughout the school. In the UK, ask for Keep Safe to be taught.
9. Ask for a whole-school anti-bullying policy to be implemented.
10. In Ireland, ask for Sticks & Stones Theatre Company to be brought to the school, and for a survey by questionnaire to be done. This will bring the problem into the open, which is particularly useful if the principal denies that there is a bullying problem in the school.

11. Ask for the school to bring in the (Irish) Red Cross Society schools officers, the Garda/Police juvenile-liaison officers and video, the Fire Brigade schools officers, and drugs advisory, smoking, alcohol and diet experts.
12. Ask for the school to take part in Mental Health Association of Ireland debates.
13. Ask for school pupils to be given projects and competitions on bully-related topics. Suggestions include artwork, song, drama, dance or essays.
14. Arrange parent–teacher(–pupil) meetings to discuss the problem of bullying and to plan how to counter it. Book videos/audios/books/leaflets/experts for this meeting.
15. Use the media – write or phone to local newspapers, radio stations and TV.
16. Offer to help – the help of parents is essential in countering bullying.
20. Keep a diary and incident book.
21. Obtain Barnardo's Child and Family Directory.
22. Get a copy of the CAPP booklet *Stay Safe: A Parents' Guide*. See the booklist and resource guide at the back of this book for more information.

Personality Types

EACH of us is a mix of the following personality types, but in each of us one particular type is dominant:

Type A cares most about achievements.
Type B cares most about emotions.
Type C cares most about enjoyment.

The poor Type C is seldom left to enjoy life in peace; there is always a Type A nagging them to achieve more and a Type B exhorting them to be sympathetic, caring, selfless and helpful. The Type C doesn't enjoy being nagged and exhorted, and so tries being selfless and achieving to see if they enjoy that. In the BBC2 series *Red Dwarf,* Rimmer, Lister and Cat are A, B and C respectively.

The best examples of personality behaviours can be summed up as follows:

Type A: 'You must work for success.'
Type B: 'Success without heart is empty.'
Type C: 'Life is wonderful.'

However, at the other end of the scale, the personality types display negative attitudes:

Type A: 'Life is a rat race.'
Type B: 'Life is a vale of tears.'
Type C: 'Life owes me more.'

This is all very relevant to bullying, because those who are strongly of one particular type may find it hard to understand the views and attitudes of those of another. This can lead to a lack of sympathy and harshness of judgement, which may be expressed in unkind bullying ways, especially where there is a conflict of interests. For resolution of conflict it is necessary to be able to see another person's point of view. Also, if the person you are dealing with is strongly typical of one of these types, A, B or C, you will find it advantageous to take this into account, whereas if you refuse to adapt your approach according to their leanings, type or beliefs, your progress, if any, will be rocky.

Suppose your employee is often late for work and tired. Don't be a bully by yelling at her, stopping her wages, demoting or sacking her out of hand, and don't let her bully you by making you put up with her poor punctuality and lack of verve. Find out why she is late. If she is a type B, it may be because she is spending so much time looking after the needs of others in which case you should take the line that she has duties also to herself and to you.

However, if your Type C is late and tired because of parties and excursions, you could point out to her that work obligations take priority over leisure activities.

If your late and tired employee is Type A, she is probably holding down two jobs or is working towards a better job elsewhere. If you don't want to lose her, consider a discussion about her time-keeping with the possibility of promotion tied to greater commitment to the company.

From your own personal point of view, a little self-analysis considering the three personality types might help you to take a conscious decision to become a more rounded, complete and integrated person. For example, if you are mainly Type A, you might be happier if you had warmer relationships. Are you ever accused of being impatient and unsympathetic, arrogant and opinionated, or of putting work before family and friends? Do you unwind and enjoy yourself regularly or at all?

Are you Type B? Do you overemphasise sentiment and emotions, wallowing in them perhaps, and does this make you a tad humourless, less competent and effective, less fun and less fulfilled than you and other people think you can be?

Are you Type C? As suggested above, you can silence your critics and fulfil your desire for pleasure by extending the range of things that give you pleasure – adding to them achievement, successes and receiving thanks for your kindness. Don't change too much – we need people who say 'Life feels good.' Life is not valued enough.

Recognising the personality types of children in your charge can help you to guide them so that they grow up fairly well balanced. For motivation, all types respond well to teaching by role-models; they will work to emulate those they really admire. Teaching a Type A requires only good-quality teaching, as they are always motivated to achieve (although of course a regular 'Well done' is always necessary). The Type B needs to feel valued as a feeling, intuitive person, and can be motivated to learn for reasons of pride, idealism or keen interest in the subject matter. Type B needs more praise than the other personality types, and is more distressed by hassle, scorn and the need to defend the value of their work.

The Type C, at least at the beginning, has to be given motivation that makes sense to a Type C and, as indicated above, that is not the same as for Type A or B. When the Type C is of school age, she takes more persuading than the others that she will be glad later on in life that she learned the school lessons and passed the exams. If the work can be made enjoyable it is easier for the Type C, whereas an A will work as long as this brings them success, and a B is prepared to suffer for a worthwhile cause.

Do not take these principles to extremes – remember, we are all a mix of types and generally achieve balance with maturity.

Play

LIKE laughter, play is natural, enjoyable, very important and necessary. Like humour, it should be taught in order to promote good relationships, good health, variety, diversity, choice and shared interests. Learning through play helps the pupil to associate learning with the positive factors such as enjoyment, progress, competition and cooperation, rules and methods, coaching, and matter-of-fact acceptance that failures and mistakes are part of the process. Play is an essential part of developing and maintaining well-adjusted people for whom bullying is unthinkable – the ideal goal of teachers everywhere.

Bullying manifests itself through play in many ways.

Bullies disrupt others' play by interruptions of various kinds; by destroying playthings, gear, premises, play areas, sports grounds et cetera; by scaring the players off. Sneering is always an effective, easy way to bully. Bullies will sneer at the game for being babyish or unsuitable for boys/girls. They sneer at the players for poor performance, for being unfit, for having the 'wrong' kind of body or clothes (especially shoes), or for the rules they are using, especially if the players have adapted the rules to accommodate the features of their group and play area. Bullies use exclusion to flaunt their power and hurt those excluded.

Bullies may cheat by pretending they've satisfied the conditions to win; by changing the rules so the victim never wins; by exclusion of anyone more likely to win; by using drugs or tampering with equipment; by sending false messages so that victims go to the wrong place or arrive at the wrong time.

Play is not war. Relationships should be competitive and friendly. Bullies change these standards, demanding that players become aggressive and unfriendly, to the point of calling conversation 'fraternising with the enemy' and making that a reason to ostracise the 'guilty' party.

Bullies use any gathering as an excuse for violence – at a soccer match this may take the form of supporters' hooliganism.

Bullies use people's ability in a very limited set of games to label them as great or useless in general, and will blame one player for the failure of a whole team. In some schools pupils are valued solely on their ability in one sport. That is now, fortunately, changing.

Bullies put players through sadistic training sessions.

Bullies associate alcohol with play.

Some bullies use sports for snobbery, by boasting about doing what others can't afford, by excluding from the inner circle of 'friends' those who can't afford the expensive activity, or by using the activity as an excuse for isolating someone at school: 'We don't mix because we have different interests.'

Countering Bullying in Play

• Make the correct attitudes explicit.

• Help the players to get the habit of friendly competition.

• Discuss the above forms of bullying in games, so that any bullying is recognised at once and stopped before damage is done.

• Have very stiff penalties for bad behaviour.

• Have as much security as possible to prevent assault, vandalism, theft or arson.

• Help all to rejoice in each other's good fortune while stamping out any sign of snobbery, sneering or exclusion.

• Teach all to admire achievements while keeping a sense of proportion. Excitement is one thing, fanaticism another.

• A good coach has knowledge, patience and perseverance, and helps and encourages the players. A coach needs to be able to analyse and give intelligible explanations. Any play should promote good health and fitness. There should be good atmosphere and good motivation.

• If adults play with children as if all are equals, they will help establish good play habits which the children can continue. In some schools the tradition is so long established that sixth-class children teach the first- and second-class children how to play the games, and the adults need only supervise. To get it started, you need adults to teach every class and to teach the older children how to teach others. The adults need to play with the children for the first six weeks or so, with some refresher courses every term. Junior and senior infants usually have a separate play time or play area, so they always need the teacher's example to learn to play happily together.

(See also **Games**.)

Rehabilitation

REHABILITATION is about restoring good health and good behaviour. It is not easy to make a full recovery from the damage done by bullying, but even a small effort will produce some improvement. The people who can help are family, friends, teachers, counsellors, psychologists, psychotherapists, voluntary organisations, club members, and, for believers, God and God's servants.

In the past some people used to say, 'The kids doing the bullying are OK, it is the victim who can't cope,' and send the victim off to see a specialist of some sort. Other people said, 'It is the bullies' behaviour which is anti-social,' and punished the bullies. The bully-victims, who displayed both bullying and victim behaviour, were treated as both victims and bullies. Even now you will sometimes meet attitudes which are inconsistent and unfair. However, if you or those close to you are suffering from a bullying problem, you have every incentive to read on and to try at least some of the measures suggested for the rehabilitation of a bully, a victim or a bully-victim.

Let us consider the bully first, as there can't be victims of bullying if nobody ever bullies.

Rehabilitating a Bully

A few of those who bully have never been victims of bullying or abuse, so they are not passing on their hurt, doing to others what has been done to hurt them. Instead they are self-centred, doing what they want without considering the rights or feelings of others. They may be quite happy and pleasant, as long as they get exactly what they want and everything goes the way they want it to go.

If they are attractive, talented and clever, good at showing pleasure and appreciation and at making their demands seem like reasonable requests, bullies like these may be indulged for many years, not just by their parents but by everyone else as well. These bullies are accomplished not only at making demands, but also at clever manipulation and, especially, at crushing challengers. 'This town ain't big enough for the both of us.' They will not brook opposition. 'Be my slave or be destroyed.' They believe they are superior; they enjoy wielding power, including the power to give rewards which they, and others, believe shows they are generous. They deliberately crush rivals and punish those who do not obey their commands. They also cause a lot of distress – which they do not notice – to many victims of their bullying behaviour.

If the distress it causes is pointed out to them, some bullies like this will change a specific behaviour. Some will say, 'Tough! Who cares? Not me.' Some enjoy their victims' pain and fear.

Rehabilitation of most bullies is possible, especially when they are children. What is difficult is establishing that it is necessary – bullies are often admired and considered popular leaders, especially if their family is powerful and influential. If your boss is this sort of bully, it is doubtful whether you can initiate rehabilitation – you can, however, use existing legislation, diplomacy and assertiveness to limit the boss's power to bully and the distress his bullying can cause. When you are dealing with colleagues, partners or children, far more can be done to make them examine their behaviour and choose to change it. It is necessary to convince them that the actions which are causing distress really are bullying, that bullying is wrong, and that you don't like it and that you are going to do something about it. All this means that they, the bullies must change some of their behaviour, attitudes and beliefs.

If you are dealing with adult bullies, you should get as much help and as many allies as possible. Alcoholics Anonymous is very helpful, even if alcohol is not the problem, as you can learn not to be an enabler and how to confront the bully with the effects of his/her behaviour. All the resources mentioned in this book are worth trying for practical help, support and advice, and to boost your morale.

If the bully is your child, make it clear that you give her things and service because you love her have the responsibility of caring for her and bringing her up, not because she issues commands and demands, and makes a fuss till you obey. Tell children what to do and what to say, and praise them when they are well-behaved, kind, considerate, loving, helpful, sharing, sensitive, sympathetic and compassionate. Keep making it clear that abuse is wrong. Develop the caring side of a child's nature by providing them with role-models and by praising them for being caring. Tell fairytales and stories like 'The Good Samaritan' to show how important it is to care for others and to be sensitive to how they feel. Enrol them in societies which offer voluntary service to prevent and alleviate human suffering, such as the Red Cross.

It is a good idea to agree contracts with the ex-bully, offering rewards for keeping to new standards of behaviour and penalties for breaking them. If you want this to work, set attainable targets. For some children there must be a good mark for every period of five minutes for which they behaved well, with a commendation for every day with X number of good marks and a little prize for Y good days or Z good marks. This has to start with 'Let's see how many you manage the first week. Then we want to see some progress every week over the previous week.' The child has the responsibility for making the contracts, keeping to their terms and keeping a record of progress – all of which is agreed with and monitored by supervisors.

You could try out the ideas for using videos, and for classroom management, which are suggested in this book. Mediation skills, and everything to do with valuing ourselves and others, are also useful tools for rehabilitating a bully.

Rehabilitating the Victims

'The bullies robbed me of a normal childhood.' 'I didn't experience the fun other teenagers take for granted.' 'There isn't any camaraderie at work, only slagging, criticism or isolation.' 'My life's not worth living.'

Some victims never become bullies, never pass on the aggression that they receive. When they come home, they don't slam the door, or flare up at the least thing, or do any of the other tiresome things bully-victims do. But their unhappiness tears the hearts of those who care about them. Their loss of confidence and self-esteem, their preoccupation with their problem, and any sign of depression or poor health become a constant worry as well as a great sadness. Usually the victims of bullying look for reassurance, consolation and an understanding sympathetic ear, all of which demands drain and strain those who love them. Parents, in particular, can feel at their wits' end.

The first thing to do is to tackle any ongoing bullying. If the problem is neighbourhood bullying speak to the bullies, their parents, the residents' association committee, the neighbourhood watch co-ordinator, the community gardaí, the local doctors, librarians, school principals, parish church officials and any other local resource. Also, organise protection for the victim, so that she won't be attacked because she is alone.

If the bullying is taking place at school, make an appointment with the principal, and use the list of suggestions contained in the chapter *Parents of a Bullied Schoolchild.*

If the problem is one of workplace bullying, read this book and *Bullying at Work* by Andrea Adams, and follow such advice in these as seems appropriate.

Next, whatever the age of the victim, try to have a peaceful, comfortable atmosphere at home and to include the following: a fragrance that makes you feel good, such as the smell of baking; the colour pink (it is both cheering and calming); feel-good music; clean, fresh air but no draughts; a comfortable temperature, not too hot or too cold; daylight in daytime, firelight, candlelight, lamplight at night; enough space to relax, sitting or reclining. Avoid anything abrasive or smothering. If possible, have a pet. A pet is wonderfully therapeutic, hence PAT, Pets As Therapy.

Victims need a sympathetic ear. They also need to hear stories similar to their own, with the clear message that it is the bullies who cause the problems and that there is good reason to hope that things will soon get better, just as they did for nearly all the victims of bullying in the stories. Because bullying makes the victims tense and stressed, it is helpful to do exercises which will make them calm, comfortable, peaceful and tranquil. Many techniques such as yoga, meditation or tai-chi can be learned at classes or at home. Exercises to build physical fitness – such as walking, weightlifting, dancing or running – are very good for your health and give a feeling of personal power, wellbeing and energy. Making music, whether by singing or playing, alone or in choirs or groups, lifts the spirits. Other creative work such as drama, painting, crafts, dressmaking, cooking or writing, have benefits similar to music-making, and also bring with them the self-esteem gained from achievement.

Love and affection are tremendously important. Laughter, especially spontaneous, happy laughter, is good for you (*see* **Videos**), and also indicates that you are on the road to recovery. When a victim has completely lost his sense of humour, the situation is serious. Look at the diet. Is it healthily balanced? Should they have a tonic, vitamins or mineral supplements? A physical check-up with your GP and a session with a counsellor are advisable. Also, use other resources and the suggestions in this book.

Many victims are full of anger at the constant and continued abuse and injustice that is spoiling their lives. They need a safety-valve to let off steam, one which does not make matters worse. Some people write it all down, venting their feelings on paper; some punch cushions, tear up newspapers, scrub out a cupboard, cut the hedge, walk, play squash, draw or visualise imaginary poetic justice, watch satirical programmes, dance, slash the tops off nettles, throw stones at rocks ... and so on. Others make matters worse by overeating, skipping meals, exhausting themselves by doing too much and depriving themselves of rest, relaxation, sleep and comfort, getting drunk, using drugs like Valium, talking incessantly and repetitively, or moping.

Rehabilitation involves persuading the victim to give up what is harming them, as well as encouraging them to do what will restore good health and happiness. If the victim has a hobby or interest, it is a good idea to join a club or class associated with that interest. Victims often think of joining a club or class to make friends and are frequently disappointed; whereas if they join from interest, they benefit from developing that interest, and nine times out of ten will make friends as well, gradually and without trying too hard – most friendships do develop gradually from shared experience.

At some stage, anybody and everybody – not only victims – should make a list of priorities and aspirations, and set about achieving some of these. School guidance counsellors, other counsellors, staff at information centres and others can help you to decide what goals appeal to you, which of these are feasible, which to choose and which approach would best suit you

Victims often need a lot of help and encouragement to do anything, because their self-confidence and zest for life have been damaged so much. It is a little easier working with children, because you can insist that they do school lessons and you can send them to several activities for a term or two to see if they like them or are good at them. If they like an activity, it gives them joy, which is necessary for rehabilitation. If they are good at it, it gives them achievement, which boosts self-confidence and self-esteem. You can also insist that they come on outings, learn to play games, learn to bake and so on. It is a good idea to invite pleasant children to come and play with yours. Also, take yours to parks or beaches where they may get on very well with children who are complete strangers and so not under the influence of the local bullies.

With adult victims, you might insist that they see a doctor, but mostly you must use the gentle art of persuasion and thoughtful gestures of affection.

Rehabilitating Bully-Victims

The bully-victim (*see* **Bully-Victims**) is the most difficult of all to rehabilitate.

Let us look at a bully-victim called Katy, who is eight

years old. Katy's parents are worried about her because she is unhappy; she whinges and complains, often misbehaves, has difficulty with her school lessons and is unpopular at school. Why can't she be good, happy, diligent and popular when she has loving parents, a good home, all she needs and lots of advantages?

They've tried talking to Katy to find out what her problems are: 'You're well able to do that dance, so why did you do it all wrong?'; 'You knew the right answer, why did you giggle and give the wrong answer?'; 'You were in time for school – why did you dawdle in the cloakroom and walk into the classroom late?'; 'Why did you pull the cat's tail?'. They get unhelpful answers like 'I was cross at missing my favourite TV programme'; 'I like winding you up.' They have tried to help her to behave sensibly instead of always making bad things worse, for example: 'Wash your hands the first time you're told, don't aggravate me by having to be told ten times before you do it.'

However, this type of behaviour means that Katy's parents are attending to the symptoms of bullying without tackling the root cause of the disease – which is ineffective, but still better than just hoping that Katy will 'learn sense' when she's older.

Suggested course of action: either one parent sits down to talk with Katy in peace while the other looks after the other children, or both parents talk to Katy while someone else gives them a couple of hours' peace. Katy's parents should establish first that they love her very much, irrespective of her behaviour and achievements, and then explain that parents have lots of emotions and Katy affects these – parents want to feel comfortable and happy with and about their children, rather than anxious, angry and despairing; they want to feel proud of their achievements rather than disappointed and ashamed; they need to be appreciated with sincerity, for example 'Thanks for that delicious dinner' rather than 'I don't like this – do I have to eat it?' Katy loves her parents; they should try to persuade her to show that love by trying to make them happy, proud and appreciated.

Next it is important to establish that at present Katy is unhappy, and her own behaviour is making matters worse. The primary causes of unhappiness, such as jealousy of sisters or brothers, bullies at school or in the neighbourhood, bouts of ill health, wanting things beyond reach, can be helped by open, honest discussion; the secondary causes, which result from bad behaviour, can be removed completely by policies of determined effort and mutual encouragement. These include learning to do well at all school lessons and at several hobbies, plus learning patterns of behaviour to cope with relationships with adults and children.

Katy has to accept authority while being allowed to express her point of view. Most of the time, parents and teachers must be obeyed. Katy has to learn to be obedient while knowing she should make value judgements and, under certain circumstances, may, even sometimes must, say 'No' to any adult. At present Katy is not obedient; she does not follow a teacher's instructions either at once or to the best of her ability. She needs to learn pleasure at doing things well without having to be praised every time she does well.

She needs to stop attention-seeking acting-out behaviour: for example, at the moment, instead of saying 'I've something really important to tell you, Mummy' and then waiting for a suitable time to talk, she says nothing much at first but is bursting to tell, and ends up acting out her frustration at not getting an opportunity to tell soon enough. The acting out takes various forms, such as knocking over stands of tins in the supermarket – 'If this supermarket didn't exist, I could be telling my news' – or standing on her mother's feet and pulling at her jacket – 'If Mummy wasn't shopping and talking to shop people and friends, I could be telling my news.'

She needs also to stop distancing pretence and acting-in behaviour: for example, at the moment, instead of saying, 'I'm upset and angry because you were ten minutes late collecting me from school', Katy does various forms of acting-in so that her parents feel and express the concern she felt she deserved but without knowing the real cause. The acting-in might include: 'I don't want any dinner, I've a tummy-ache', 'I can't do my sums. I don't understand them', or 'I can't sleep in these pyjamas. They are too uncomfortable.' As with crying wolf, there is a danger that Katy's parents will become unsympathetic and pay less and less heed to her complaints. It is very important for Katy to understand this, and the story of the little boy who cried wolf is a good start.

Katy needs to build the self-confidence to be open and honest, though not in a rude way. She needs to build her trust in the goodwill and good sense of parents and teachers. She needs to build her own self-esteem with achievements. Ten minutes' tutoring every so often to help her to master one thing at a time is often the best way over difficulties or mental blocks. Because Katy has behavioural problems she will learn best with one-to-one teaching. This is true also if a child has a special educational difficulty such as dyslexia. A good tutor will also teach her how to study on her own, an invaluable ability and one which strengthens self-reliance, self-confidence and self-honesty. A computer, allowing no arguments and no cheating, is good too.

While it is good advice to parents to say, 'Listen to your children. Hear what they are not saying [read between the lines]. Acquire listening skills', it is a bit one-sided. Probably the hardest thing, but the most beneficial, is for Katy to learn to talk to a parent with total honesty. Unless a person is unloved, starving or crippled, their circumstances are not the major cause of their unhappiness – it is their attitude and behaviour which make them happy or unhappy. The unburdening which comes from a heart-to-heart is not to be confused with griping and complaining. Katy probably needs to be helped to understand the difference.

Making contracts for specific things is the way to get Katy's rehabilitation started in a practical way. This might involve Katy agreeing to do certain things (like obeying a teacher's instructions at once), or to be tutored for short sessions to achieve specific goals (such as learning to polka, to recite a short poem or to play a card game). She will have certain rights defined (such as the right to be told in advance what is expected of her) and is assured these will be respected.

Good books and TV programmes help to establish that her parents' standards and ideals are general and not just their own hare-brained notions; they also show that Katy's experience is indeed very limited. Katy needs to separate things into *good*, *bad* and *a matter of taste*. Much misery is caused by incorrect classification of these.

Who decides what Katy does?

Katy's parents? If this is the case, her parents should tell her why they have decided on a particular course of action, and she should be allowed to discuss the details with them. Katy herself? Here Katy decides what to do and her parents have some input and set limits. Katy's peers? If this is the case, then disaster looms. 'You must wear this, eat that, play the latest fashion fad.' Katy becomes their puppet.

As a result of their talk, Katy's parents decide to enrol her for piano lessons, and say to her, 'We think everyone should be able to read music and play a musical instrument, so we have decided to send you to piano lessons. You will take piano lessons until you have passed Grade Two. After that, if you do not like playing the piano, you will be allowed to stop.'

Here the child is given a good reason for the activity. She is not bound to do the activity for a very long time – four years at the most – and eventually she will have a choice about the activity. She has no choice now, so it is pointless to make a fuss. She must pass the exams, so it is pointless to prolong the agony by doing badly on purpose. The child is not told to get Honours, however, and so does not have too much expected of her. Her parents must make passing the exams possible by cooperating with the piano teacher. Katy sees that they do their duty and keep their word. She tells her peers, 'My parents say I have to', so her peers give up pressuring her to revolt. The child benefits from learning, achieving, merited praise and cooperating with her parents. She learns to trust and appreciate her parents' good sense, and that the phrase 'My parents say ... and that's that' silences her peers – something which comes in useful time and again, giving Katy confidence in her ability to cope with peer pressure.

Hopefully the child learns to talk to her parents about things directly, honestly, straightforwardly, rather than 'acting-in' or 'acting-out' her problems. She also learns that power-struggles need to be solved at the conference table, with negotiation and acceptance of terms. Parents must be the bosses, because they are responsible for her welfare. Children and parents must each have their needs and feelings treated with sympathy and respect.

Having learnt the importance of all that, Katy will be less likely to want to be a bully or to be subservient to bullies. She'll be able to say, 'What gives you the right to tell me what to wear? My parents and I together decide things like that.'

All the advice about rehabilitating bullies and victims is worth trying for bully-victims. Other forms of behaviour modification may be used. Psychologists can help to draw up programmes to restore or establish acceptable behaviour in disruptive or disturbed children. Full rehabilitation depends on love, rewarding good behaviour, not permitting bad behaviour, giving the child some responsibility for their own progress, and on keeping plans and instructions clear and simple.

Experience suggests that full rehabilitation always takes more than a year, but that children can have nearly recovered in about a year. However, if a child is bullied for years, then, although they may have fully recovered by the time they are grown up, the memories of childhood bullying are likely to flood back if they are bullied again, and that will upset them a lot. Usually they make a quick recovery from such an upset, but it explains how sometimes people will react very differently to similar situations in the short term.

(*See* **Avoiding Bullying.**)

Research

'Few topics are more thoroughly obscured by unsound information, contradictory religious and cultural beliefs, and illogical thinking than human reproduction and child-rearing practices. These subjects are the source of the fiercest ... clashes between comparative biologists ... physicians ... religious dogmatists and political pragmatists'.
Caroline Pond, *New Scientist*, 26 November 1994.

CaB receives many requests for information. Most are from people with a bullying problem, but a fair number have always been from folk who, for some reason, are doing research on bullying for articles, projects, essays, speeches, theses or dissertations. In the early days of CaB these letters came from journalists, children, teachers and student-teachers. Now the letter-writers include psychologists, doctors, nurses, workers in childcare, police officers, prison officers, union officials, personnel officers, and students of business management, consumer studies, counselling, community studies, self-defence, assertiveness training, equality, safety and other areas.

Some of these researchers want to base their theories and recommendations on traditional rules of thumb, long-held opinions, a couple of personal experiences and 'gut-feelings'. You'll get away with that in an essay, discussion or class debate, but this kind of subjective thinking will not pass muster as scientific research. Scientific research has to be as objective as possible. For example, all things being equal, if you have three bananas and you throw one away, you now have two bananas. Opinion doesn't enter into it. Or a doctor may think you have osteoporosis, but if your bone scan shows that you do not, she will accept that objective evidence. In the face of such evidence, opinion, even opinion based on experience, does not count.

Some scientific findings apply right across the board: 'All

humans need air.' Some will come out as percentages and their accuracy will depend on the sample: 'Some humans can see and some are blind.' Where there are causes and cures, scientific surveys can evaluate the effectiveness of any course of action taken, and these should influence policy decisions. For example, non-contact sports injuries were greatly reduced when exercises to increase flexibility were introduced, and eradicating a species of snail from water supplies resulted in fewer cases of blindness in parts of Africa.

Simple definitions of subjective and objective are: what we think and feel is subjective; what we measure with instruments is objective. Our observations can be very accurate, while our opinions of them vary according to our situation and experience; two people might describe a meal in identical terms except that one calls it 'a simple meal', the other, 'a feast'. Examples such as this should warn us not to jump to conclusions about why people behave as they do, and remind us that our mood colours our perceptions.

When one is unusually vulnerable emotionally, a level of bullying that was previously a minor annoyance can become unbearable. Watch out for this when someone in your care is bereaved or ill, or has new problems at home such as illness in the family, someone out of work, parents separating, or a close friend or sibling emigrating.

Now let us consider scientific evidence of incidences of bullying, and the interpretation of that evidence. The collection and selection of evidence is very important – 'It is a poor theory that can't gather a few facts to support it.' If your results contradict conventional wisdom, then you will need to gather far more evidence as proof and you will need evidence to argue convincingly against the previous theories. This has been the case for those researching bullying, for there were many myths to expose and dispel – myths such as 'Words can never hurt me', 'Girls don't bully' and 'If you ignore bullying it will stop'. It used to be easy to blind people with science, but now there is a general resistance to believing scientific experts. As always, a little knowledge is a dangerous thing – it is easier to lead by the nose someone who has done enough study to follow some of what the expert is saying.

For example, because some bullies and some victims come from broken homes or families with huge problems, many people were easily convinced by experts who told them, with plausible arguments illustrated by true stories, that all bullying is caused by serious family problems. This contributed to these people's reluctance to admit that they had any kind of bullying problem, and supported those teachers who said that bullying is not a school-based problem, as well as all those, including these teachers, who said, 'Bullying comes from the home. I blame the parents.' To counter this theory, it was necessary to show that a large proportion of bullies and victims come from families with no more than the usual number of problems, that bullying behaviour can be caused by factors outside the home, and that the effects of bullying on the victim cause new problems for the victim's family. Also shown was that, no matter where it arises, bullying can be tackled successfully at school. Thankfully, research in this area has now been done in many centres in many countries, and we are now at the stage where surveys can be done to verify results and to highlight individual idiosyncrasies, rather than to establish the basic facts about bullying. It is to be hoped that this speeds up the work that needs to be done to tackle bullying in the workplace, in neighbourhoods and in institutions.

The need for objectivity means that researchers must accept only the hardest of evidence, though in some areas these rules are so strict that valuable information is excluded, thus impeding progress. Complex structures and creatures, such as humans, ecologies and economies, have so many aspects, attributes and variables that it is necessary to be selective as regards evidence, and the results of research will be more or less useful and valid according to the decisions taken by the researcher about what selection to study. For example, if the designer of an IQ (Intelligence Quotient) test chooses to use topics likely to be found in the background knowledge of white children living in New York, such children are likely to achieve higher scores than country-folk, African-Americans or Hispanics. To be objectively fair and scientific, IQ tests must be based on shared experience, including education. Similarly, selection can skew results from investigations into illnesses, drug abuse and crime, or into any aspect of bullying.

I have met many people who believe that bullying never happens in fee-paying schools. Others believe it happens only in boarding schools. The many surveys prove it happens in all schools, but can be eliminated almost completely by having an excellent school policy implemented effectively by staff with the cooperation of pupils and parents. The fundamental component of such a policy is genuine, mutual respect. The most essential element is a printed code of conduct, ethics and procedures. The key person, if it is all to work, is the school principal, who in turn can be influenced for good or ill by the staff, pupils and parents. Sometimes it takes only one child to prompt a parent to persuade a principal to introduce a complete anti-bullying policy to the school. Some principals respond readily to reasonable requests; others make improvements only when several parents move their children to a better-run school. Some treat their staff better in response to appeals to their better nature; others change because of representations by union representatives, Department of Education inspectors, or, indeed, Health and Safety Authority Inspectors.

These general principles apply right across the board: atmosphere and standards are set by the person(s) in charge, and these persons in authority can be influenced to improve matters. Even one person can start what eventually makes a big difference.

Responsibility

THE concept of responsibility is of tremendous importance in life. We all need to know that we can rely on people to do the things they have agreed to do. As has been discussed earlier, in the section on **Blame**, we all have rights; therefore we all have responsibilities.

When establishing responsibility, we should ask the following questions:

- 'Who is responsible?'/'Whose job is it?'
- 'Do they know it's their job?'
- 'Do they know what the job entails?'
- 'Is it sole or shared responsibility?'
- 'Who carries the can?'
- 'Does the buck stop here?'
- 'Who decided who was to be in charge of that?'
- 'Were they given any training or left to sink or swim, to test their calibre? Were their questions answered with, 'Find out', or worse?'
- 'Does anybody know?'

These are important questions and sometimes the answers are surprising. 'Who is responsible for this success?' should lead to giving credit where it is due. 'Who is responsible for this mess?' will lead to apportioning blame.

Then there are these comments expressing admiration and exasperation: 'She is very responsible – always tries to do her duty and usually succeeds.' 'She is very irresponsible – giddy, careless, forgetful, unrepentant, defies attempts to make blame stick; complaints are to her like water off a duck's back.' Of particular relevance to bullying, consider the following.

Prevention and rehabilitation

Praise for being responsible helps to build self-esteem, especially as the praise is generally heartfelt and the person giving the praise is also giving gratitude. When giving responsibility, remember that 'some fail because they can't do', and be sure that the person is capable of what you are asking of them. Be sure to give any necessary training, supervision, back-up and encouragement. Others fail because they don't want to bother. You need to find out why. They may have been put off by past experiences; perhaps the rewards, incentives and appreciation are too small, even non-existent. Perhaps some bullies are even undermining your efforts by telling their victim: 'You're missing out', 'You're being used', 'It's not fair to me', 'You're being very selfish', or, worse, threatening them.

Rehabilitation and reform

When dealing with someone who has a history of bad behaviour, it is of paramount importance to ensure that he learns to take responsibility for his actions. To be rehabilitated, the ex-bully must feel in charge and in control of his own actions. He must practise honesty. He must not 'get let off' because of extenuating circumstances, but he must also get sympathy, compassion and as much help as possible to solve his problems and alleviate his pain.

We must all learn to take increasing responsibility for ourselves, including our general health and wellbeing, as those who have adopted a self-help approach to coping with afflictions such as ME or arthritis exemplify.

Rights

CHILDREN have the right to be happy and safe.

Children have the right not to be bullied or abused in any way. Nobody has the right to bully.

It is an unpopular truth that the only rights we have which come with a 100 per cent guarantee are those spiritual rights given us by God, or by virtue of being human. These are the only ones which cannot be taken away from us by some misfortune, by people or by happenings outside our control. These days it sometimes seems as if most people believe that they have a right to everything they want, and that if they do not have what they desire they are being deprived of it unfairly. These false hopes and expectations lead to chips on shoulders, nursed grievances, and apportioning of guilt and blame all over the place.

Legislation and constitutions attempt to set out and affirm basic rights: for example, the right to life, liberty and the pursuit of happiness; the right to *liberté, egalité, fraternité*; the right to free education, a basic minimum wage, gender equity. But rights exist only in so far as they are implemented and enforced by law, and the belief that things are otherwise causes great and utterly useless anger, distress and long-term misery.

Instead of protecting avowed 'inalienable' rights, communities tend to live by unwritten rules such as 'Don't make trouble', 'Don't tell tales', 'Put the boot in', 'Protect your own', 'Don't rock the boat', 'If you can't beat them, join them', 'The weak go to the wall', 'If you don't like it here, go and live somewhere else' and 'If you break the law, you must pay the penalty'.

People harassed in their homes often say, 'Surely we have a right to some peace and quiet. What do we pay taxes for?' We pay taxes because the government of the country has the right to levy taxes – a right which seems to have gone to their collective heads. However, they certainly have to spend money on tax collectors and to wield a heavy stick to ensure that most taxes get paid. Like the rest of us, they have to spend a bit of time, energy and money to get what they have a right to. In fact, if we really want our rights, we must affirm, defend and uphold the rights of others, especially of others in our own family, street, school, town and so on, as best we can.

All rights carry responsibilities. Rights and responsibilities are two sides of the same coin.

Sport

BULLIES attack sport, as they attack other worthwhile things, by denigration and corruption.

From the outside the sport is attacked as ridiculous and possibly foreign, while anyone engaged in it is also ridiculous, strange, weird and different, and, of course, deserving of being bullied. Even if the sport is played at school, a distinction can be drawn between those who choose to play and those who play only when they have to.

From the inside there are, as always, two distinct forms of bullying: the form where everything but the sport itself and its standards are attacked; and secondly the systematic destruction of all the admirable attributes of the sport itself.

Among the tenets that used to make the sportsperson's character admirable were fair play, respecting the rules, not seeking unfair advantage, respecting competitors, working to achieve strength and skill, doing one's best, being a good team member. But these seem to be under threat by bullying behaviour.

In 1994 there were newspaper reports of this bullying canker in cricket, soccer and rugby, among other sports. The expression 'That's not cricket' has been dealt what may be a death-blow by revelations about cricket-ball seams unpicked or deliberately flawed with dirt in world test matches. In rugby, the horrid atmosphere was summed up in August 1994 by Jan Pieter Engelbrecht, manager of the South African team preparing to tour in Wales and Scotland. He said: 'We are spending millions of pounds promoting the game – but violence is killing it.' As reported by John Redmond in the *Evening Press*, 'This summer has been a nightmare for the image of rugby, with a succession of serious injuries being inflicted and incidents taking place that have marred the profile of the game.' Worldwide examples are given, mainly of 'stamping'. Fortunately, the Irish Rugby

Football Union 'find the current trend unacceptable and they will not condone any acts of violence.'

Not so reassuring is the article in the *Weekly News* of 14 May 1994, profiling soccer player Lee Sharpe: 'I had lumps kicked out of me for a whole year during my apprenticeship at Torquay United. It turned out to be the making of me ... Cyril Knowles [manager at Plainmoor] devised a game called Murder Ball, in which the apprentices were let loose on each other in a small, enclosed concrete square ... there would be such a cloud of dust that we'd all still be hammering into each other long after the ball came bouncing out ... Boots would go flying in indiscriminately ... It certainly toughened me up. To begin with, I was taking everything and giving nothing back. I came off with dead legs, bumps, bruises and very sore shins. But after a couple of sessions, I started to realise that I had to give as much as I was getting, otherwise I wouldn't last very long.' This kind of training promotes bullying behaviour instead of sporting skill.

Sport has suffered also by being treated as if it is to be revered rather than properly valued. Believing sport to be safe and good, parents have been too ready to trust sports coaches. There have been many recent reports of child sexual abuse by sports coaches.

Bullies' propaganda also includes barriers dividing sport and arts, sport and intelligence, sport and academic prowess, dislike of sport and worthiness of success. There are countless examples to show how scurrilous and nonsensical that propaganda is, from the sporty personalities in prison cells to people like Professor J.R.R. Tolkien, author of *The Hobbit* and *The Lord of the Rings*, who captained both the debating and the football teams at school.

In short, it is entirely appropriate that two synonyms for 'bully' are 'killjoy' and 'spoilsport'.

Statistics

'There are lies, damned lies, and statistics'. Mark Twain

STATISTICS are rather like knives: tools which vary a good deal in quality, and which may be very useful or misused to cause harm. Often there may be more appropriate tools. It is often said that you can use statistics to prove whatever you want.

A popular story tells of three academics travelling by train. They notice some white sheep in a field and then a black sheep in another field and one comments, 'I see they farm both white and black sheep in this part of the country.' The second says, 'In the interests of accuracy you can only say one black sheep.' The third points out that the most they can claim to have observed was that one sheep was black on one side.

We cannot tell from this story whether they do farm both black and white sheep in that part of the country, or if the black sheep was the one exception that proves – that is, tests – the rule or generalisation that all sheep in that place are white.

Statistics as a subject is all about probability, but the word 'statistics' is generally used to mean facts and figures used as evidence.

Recently a headmaster argued that it was ridiculous to demand a whole-school policy on bullying, because the statistics in somebody's book showed that only five per cent of pupils were adversely affected by bullying in the long term. Why should the other 95 per cent waste valuable school time on anti-bullying activity? This was the sort of thing I was thinking of when, in February 1994, I wrote the following in response to a college student's 'desperate' request for statistics on bullying in Ireland:

'Few people (less than 20 per cent of teachers by July

1994) have read the *Guidelines on Countering Bullying Behaviour in Schools*, and far fewer have digested and understood them; fewer still have attempted to put the Whole-School Policy into practice. It is not so very difficult to do – as far back as 1989 school principals used CaB information and lending library of Besag's book on bullies and victims, and Kidscape material, etc. to put in place an effective whole-school policy in their own schools.

My degree is in Honours Maths and Political Economy, with Logic and English at Ordinary Level. Statistics questions were a compulsory part of the exam work. It is not, therefore, from unfamiliarity that I cast doubt on the value of statistics. It is necessary to collect some, of course, as part of highlighting a problem, but it is the discussion that precedes and results from the statistics that is effective, or not. It makes little difference whether you say that 100 per cent of adults aged thirty years have experienced and suffered inconvenience as a result of bullying in our community (true); that five per cent of those who bully a lot at school have severe problems in adult life (also true); that at least 10,000 children are suffering now as victims of school and/or neighbourhood bullying (true). Make that figure 50,000 or 100,000 and the impact is virtually the same. We count 'one person associated with me' as too many; 'one thousand in this country' as 'a lot but not my problem'; '50,000 in this country' as a lot, something should be done'; and '100 per cent of people in this country' as 'That means me and mine. So what? We're okay, it can't be that important; I'm okay, so bullying never harmed me, so it doesn't harm anyone except weaklings, *et cetera, et cetera*.

Ask the average person on the street and they still say, as the late Father Cleary did (frequently): 'Just punch the bully in the face – problem solved.'

We've a long way still to go.'

In conclusion, we must, as always, beware of throwing the baby out with the bathwater. Despite its limitations for anti-bullying work, statistical evidence is both useful and necessary for basic information on which to base anti-bullying policy, supported by funding for the preparation, introduction and refinement of anti-bullying methods and tools, and for the evaluation of the effectiveness of these to solve and alleviate problems.

Stress and Burnout

BULLYING is a cause of stress, and where bullying causes overwork, it may also cause burnout. Because burnout and stress cause irritability, impatience and loss of sympathy, caring and compassion, they in turn cause bullying.

Clearly, it is necessary to break this vicious circle by tackling all three problems: bullying, stress and burnout. If you find it hard to relax, to smile and to laugh naturally and normally, you may well be under stress and in the process of burnout. If this is the case, try to regard it as a temporary problem which can be overcome with help. Try to pinpoint the sources of stress, and consider how these can be removed or reduced with help and support from others. We are all interdependent, and need to be willing to give and receive help and support.

The chapter on **Rehabilitation** has many suggestions which might help.

- Try the sympathetic ear of a family member or friend;
- enjoy the company of a pet – some people have pets, but let themselves become so busy they forget to spend time with them;
- comfort and pamper yourself and give yourself a better, more nutritious and tastier diet;
- use music, entertainment and enjoyable recreation such as a good book or computer game;
- take a holiday – even if it is spent at home you will be able to rest, recuperate and enjoy life;
- relaxation tapes and exercises, meditation, yoga, dancing and swimming are all good for stress release;
- counselling by professional counsellors, or by close friends or teachers can help you to get things into perspective and to draw up a plan to make goals attainable without so much pressure. Perhaps a deadline can be

postponed; someone else may be able to take on one of your duties; maybe some activity can be discontinued for a few months till other matters have been attended to and cleared away. Ironically those in the process of burnout often take on extra tasks, such as house-decorating.

Stress is not bad in itself; it is prolonged stress which causes the damage. In her book *ME: Post-Viral Fatigue Syndrome, How to Live with It*, Dr Anne MacIntyre says that 'Stress produces an outpouring of cortisone, adrenaline and cholesterol to prepare the body for "fight or flight" – the initial arousal state.' Once the stressful situation is over, the body returns to normal. However, she states, 'repeated stressing leads to a stage of adaptation, and the arousal changes become more or less permanent.' The person appears to have adapted to the stress and to be coping, but general health declines. Symptoms include flu-like illnesses, headaches, digestive problems, sleep disturbance, high blood pressure, difficulty concentrating et cetera.

Telephone Calls - Abusive

MANY PEOPLE find these a very upsetting form of abuse.

The best response to a nuisance telephone call is to hang up. If the call is repeated, hang up and then telephone a friend or just leave the phone off the hook for five minutes. Some people advise keeping a whistle by the phone and blowing it into the receiver – this seldom works, like all tit-for-tat methods, because the caller could well ring you back and blow a whistle himself.

Serious nuisance calls should be traced. If the person calling sounds violent or mentally disturbed, contact the telephone company to make an arrangement for the calls to be traced. This may involve signing an agreement form at a police station. Many arrests have been made of persons guilty of making abusive telephone calls. You may prefer your telephone number to be ex-directory, but that won't stop nuisance calls from classmates or workmates. If you recognise the caller's voice, tell their parents or the teacher or your boss, as appropriate.

Victims of bullying can become very distraught over a nuisance telephone call. It is not a trivial matter.

Victims

THE CAUSE of bullying is the person who bullies. Regardless of whether you are attractive or not, mannerly or not, deserving of criticism or not, you do not deserve abuse.

Victims of bullying do not cause bullying, any more than victims of floods or burglary cause natural disasters or crimes. If you leave your house with windows open and nobody there, then your house is an easy target for a burglar. However, the fault is the burglar's for committing the crime. Honest folk do not steal, no matter how easy it is. It cannot be said often enough that bullying is wrong and it is the bully who is at fault.

Let me quote a sentence from a letter to CaB: 'I am doing a project and I need to know what could be the main causes of one child being picked on rather than another.' It is obvious to everybody that some people are bullied much more than others. There are two reasons for this: one is that the victim is in the same place at the same time as someone who decides to bully them; the other is that the bully is able to go on bullying the victim and continues to want to bully that person. The bully wants to bully the victim because of personal reasons such as jealousy and a desire for revenge, not always against the person but because of something that person represents, such as a particular religion, race, political persuasion or income group.

The bully wants to bully, get away with it and be able to keep on doing it, so she picks on those who are easiest to bully. Some bullies enjoy the victim's reactions, and so pick on those who get most upset, flustered, angry or fearful. Some bullies play to a crowd of sniggering sycophants and ill-natured oafs because they enjoy the acclaim.

In other words, bullies choose victims for personal reasons connected to how they themselves feel; they prefer those who are easiest to bully; and they enjoy the reaction they get from the victim and/or the onlookers.

To *rehabilitate* bullies, the important thing is to sort out the *personal reasons* they have for their bullying behaviour. That may be difficult and take a long time. However, the bullying can be stopped rather more quickly by tackling the other areas of *ease* and *reactions* – by making it very difficult for them to bully at all, by not letting them get away with it, by not letting them get the reaction they enjoy from the victim and by tackling the attitude of the crowd who used to make them feel important and clever when bullying.

It is easier to bully someone who is quiet, as they don't make a noise which gets noticed and attended to. Counteract this by teaching everybody to be self-assertive, to stand up for themselves and for each other, and to tell and keep telling if something is wrong. Give them words they can use and feel comfortable with such as, 'Hey', 'Watch it', 'Stop', 'No', 'Don't do that', 'That is mine', 'Not yet', 'Help', 'Everybody come here and help'.

It is easier to bully someone who believes that it is their fault, that she is being bullied because she is different. Counteract that by helping everybody to value themselves and others, both for the ways in which we are all the same and for the differences that make us individual and give rich variety to society. It is easier to bully somebody who has few friends, as few people will defend them. Counteract that by helping everybody to have basic social skills and tolerable behaviour, and by encouraging everybody to leap to the defence of anybody threatened with abuse.

To summarise: because of *ease of bullying* and *the reactions of the victim and the onlookers*, and in the absence of an anti-bullying policy implemented by those in authority, a bully will pick on someone if that person: does not stand up for him/herself; is passive or submissive; is tearful, whinging, anxious, whining; is rude; is very unfriendly and cold, or snarls and snaps; is too trusting and gullible; is too generous, giving rather than sharing; lacks joy, self-confidence, abilities, pride; is boastful, sneering, smug, unfair; has no words for self-assertiveness; has no one to defend him/her.

Videos

Using Them to Counter Bullying

COMBATING bullying is obviously difficult and therefore daunting. However, it is not impossible, for it has been done, and it makes sense to use methods and tools which have worked well for other people. Most people have access to a video recorder, so the use of videos is particularly easy and practical. It is also especially valuable in many ways which are described in this chapter.

When using videos there are two rules: choose one you have enjoyed yourself; and choose one appropriate for the viewers' age group. It is vital that after the showing of the video, the group leader holds a discussion session, during which the points raised by the film can be clearly discussed. By group leader I mean whoever is in charge of the video session – it may be a teacher for other teachers; pupils, parents or a youth club; or it may be a parent; committee member of any association, including a residents' association or a musical society; a personnel officer or trade union representative; in other words, anyone who decides to do this.

There are two types of video to be considered.

Videos on Bullying
These videos deal exclusively with the subject of bullying. Some are produced by anti-bullying project teams, and some are videos of TV programmes. They may include: short talks from experts giving definitions and statistics; group discussions; interviews; reconstructions of real events played out by actors; and dramas. The dramas may have been written for professional actors to perform just for the video, or principally to be performed live as part of an anti-bullying initiative. Sometimes the dramas are made up by those at

whom the anti-bullying initiative is aimed, such as a class of schoolchildren, a team of workers or a group of prisoners.

These videos can be obtained from the project teams that produced them, by recording the TV programme when it is broadcast, from anti-bullying groups and from resource centres with libraries. There are at least ten ways in which they are useful.

- Along with the growing number of books and the huge number of newspaper and magazine articles on bullying, these videos demonstrate a widespread interest and concern about this issue. Bullying is topical. But not everyone knows this. The first use of these videos is, therefore, as proof that bullying is topical.
- The videos show the current views of the issues, such as what counts as bullying. Without a consensus view of what constitutes bullying, you cannot hope to tackle it.
- They also show that most victims and bullies are not like the usual preconceived stereotypes.
- Through their use of drama and real-life stories, the videos can touch the viewer's heart. Few come away without feelings of sympathy for the victim, disgust at the bullying, and anger where any authorities made matters worse, either by doing nothing or by doing the wrong thing.
- The viewer sees the victim's distress and the bully's abuse of power, as well as the lies, denials and justifications commonly used by bullies. This helps the viewer to recognise these for what they are.
- Seeing that many cases have similar causes and consequences helps to conquer the viewer's scepticism regarding cause and effect. The evidence is convincing.
- Very importantly, the videos show that dealing with the issue is not all gloom and doom. Most programmes on bullying have shown some positive and effective ways of tackling the problem.
- Most programmes indicate how to obtain more information. This can give renewed hope to those who

previously felt that nothing could be done to improve matters.

- When shown experiences similar to their own, many people find it easier to say, 'That happened to me too', or 'I used to do that'. They feel less isolated and are able to be more open.
- When viewers realise some of their beliefs were mistaken, they are freed from the hindrance of these myths. In fact, a video is a quick and relatively painless way to dispel ignorance.

To sum up, videos on bullying increase viewers' awareness and understanding, their desire to solve bullying problems, and their ability to identify the forms of bullying affecting their group. In addition, viewers learn recommended ways to reduce the number and severity of incidents of bullying, where further information can be obtained, and that the consequences of inaction are dire.

The biggest drawback is the length of time required to see enough to get a clear overall picture. Ideally, there should be at least twelve hours' viewing time available to the group. Most people balk at more than forty minutes. There is great resistance to fulfilling this time requirement. If people don't want to watch something they switch off their attention, so it is pointless to force them to sit through more than they want. Also, if they see too much in one go, they forget most of it. To get around these difficulties, a group leader may select sections of between two and five minutes' duration and show these, with as much time for discussion in between as seems productive and useful. Unfortunately, this means highlighting problems the leader assumes are relevant. Some viewers may be inhibited by this, reluctant to air a problem that hasn't been ratified. The leader could overcome this by making comprehensive lists of all forms of bullying mentioned in the videos, and asking the group members to tick the ones of interest to them (anonymously if they wish).

When parents are informed that there is a designated teacher to whom they should make their initial reports and enquiries regarding any bullying problem, they will assume that this teacher is well informed on the subject. It would therefore be sensible for such a teacher to view as many videos on bullying as possible. This seldom happens at present, although things are improving.

Other Videos

Entertaining videos that viewers thoroughly enjoy watching can be used to combat bullying in all of the following ways and probably more besides.

As a reward for good behaviour; as entertainment, to produce a happy atmosphere; as shared experience to improve communication skills, empathy and fellow-feeling. Rewards, shared happiness and shared experience lead to fellow feeling, and form a basis for communication. Children will work for a reward, especially one they enjoy, and videos are excellent in this respect. If children enjoy something positive, they'll want to do it again, thus forming good habits and leaving less time for mischief and less desire for troublemaking.

It is easier for a child – or for anyone – if they can communicate feelings in language based on shared experience: 'It was like something out of that Laurel and Hardy film we watched' instead of just 'That was funny'. Quite a lot of children, for instance, find their younger brother or sister identifies with Chip in *Beauty and the Beast*. Teenage boys often have fellow-feeling with Spike in *Dad's Army*. And there's a lot to be said for the catchphrases that emerge from these programmes. Even simple catchphrases such as 'There's nobody here but us chickens' or 'Your wish is my command' can relieve boredom, create group unity and increase a liking for words. Children pick up words from anywhere, including videos, and they'll use them more readily when they've all heard them together while enjoying themselves.

Teachers and parents can encourage a few quotations from any source to build the children's vocabulary – this is especially important to help them to talk about feelings with clarity and understanding, and without feeling embarrassed. After reading a story, or watching a film or play, the teacher could ask, 'How do you think X felt when ...?'

In order for mediation to be successful (*see* **Mediation**), children must be able to answer the questions 'What happened?', 'How did you feel?', and 'How do you feel now?' To say, 'I felt like Cinderella when she wasn't allowed to go to the ball' can be readily understood if all have seen the scene referred to. Even if they've seen distress only on video, children will be more likely to notice it in real life, and to respond to it with compassion, if it is something that is familiar to them.

To give information about other people, their lifestyles, beliefs, feelings, abilities, standards, values and problems.

To show many ways of handling a variety of situations. Videos, as well as books and plays, also give possible solutions and ways of handling a bullying situation when it arises. The discussion point 'That worked well but would it work here in our home or school?' offers a fair chance that a suitable, sensible, effective solution will be chosen. If there is no discussion, it is likely that volatile people will choose vivid and dramatic rather than wise courses of action – partly because these have stuck in their memory. Youngsters tend to copy characters who run wildly off to disaster when upset. Point this out and list a lot of better courses of action.

To engender interest in something worthwhile, like music. Unfamiliarity breeds contempt too! If children are exposed to the arts, they will like some things at once and acquire more appreciation each time. It helps if they are guided into verbalising a little about what they liked – it strengthens the memory and reinforces the enjoyment. The teacher should focus on praising both the work that is viewed and the children's own work. It is healthy for people to use the words 'beauty' and 'beautiful'. Self-expression is so healthy, in fact, that it even boosts the immune system – and it becomes easier when there are plenty of examples to fire the imagination or even just to copy; copying builds technique till originality becomes natural.

Also, you can use a form of peer magic to influence how they value Shakespeare's plays. For example, when they were shown Russian and Chinese dancers expressing appreciation for Shakespeare's plays, saying that all educated people worldwide are familiar with the works of Shakespeare, some Dublin dance pupils' attitude instantly swung from 'Why study Shakespeare at school?' to 'Shakespeare's great'. Children – and most adults – need to identify with peers, so give them peers worth relating to. If you are lucky, the few you influence will bring the whole class with them by peer-group magic. Magic is powerful stuff, so be cautious in using it and back up its effects with sound reasons and argument. Bullies use peer pressure all the time to bad purpose; how much better to use peer pressure to limit the   bullies' power.

To engender appreciation of valuable attributes in people and things, such as courage, colour, individuality or beauty. Showing the best attributes of other countries and the most admirable members of other races is the quickest way to beat racism. Televised tributes to great achievers can be used to counter ignorant prejudice towards the activity for which the achiever is famous, and towards his or her race or sex, especially in the case of a woman in a male-dominated area. Travel documentaries, nature series, arts programmes including master classes and reviews of someone's career to date, can engender interest and appreciation.

To help engender feelings of respect for others; and to demonstrate ways of showing respect including self-respect. Consider using a series such as *Head of the Class*, or clips of achievers paying tribute to a teacher, to show that respecting your teacher is a good thing, something that many people do. Show enough to establish why the achiever is admired, as well as including the tribute to the teacher. This is effective because children want to be happy, successful and admired both now and when they are grown-up, and they instinctively emulate role-models presented to them. Also, in this case, it is necessary to counterbalance the huge number of negative messages about teachers, schools (and parents), and to moderate the influence of the many role-models who had good reason to hate school.

Everyone sees the attraction of glamour, wealth and power. However, this attraction can be counteracted by a judicious choice of viewing and reading, where there are clear distinctions made between the self-esteem based on boasting, using force and having things, and the self-esteem based on valuable skills and qualities. Equally important is the distinction between mutual respect and slavish abasement before a bully. *The Narnian Chronicles*, *The Magic Box* and *Archers Goon* are particularly good examples of exciting TV series which made these points.

To teach the worth of value judgements. In a general way, humour always helps to maintain a sense of proportion and to identify the preposterous. The Walt Disney film *Beauty and the Beast* makes several important points relevant to bullying and love. The *Kung Fu* television series tackles several abuse-related topics in each episode. Try to tackle at least one point raised in the programme in the discussion session – remember, it is useless to show videos without such a session. If you pick something you know your colleagues, neighbours, children or pupils enjoy, you can use it to discuss matters and help them to weigh issues up and decide for themselves as a matter of course. This is important – not least because bullies like fooling the gullible.

To develop a sense of humour. This is an essential part of human nature, necessary not just for fun but for survival; not just for mental health but also for physical health; not just for leisure but for a sense of proportion, a sense of the fitness of things, and for the recognition of the ridiculous and absurd, the cock-eyed and skewed, the meaningless and the distorted. Humour promotes health and counteracts bullying.

Laughter relieves stress and tension, and also produces endorphins (natural pain-killers) and antibodies to infection, in particular to the viruses and bacteria associated with colds and flus. It boosts the immune system and relieves pain. Bullying has the opposite effect. Watching funny films doesn't solve the actual aggression side of a bullying problem, but can counteract some of its effects and promote a robust resilience.

Of course, humour purely for fun is very beneficial. Young children love to laugh. Try *Mary Poppins*, especially the song 'I Love to Laugh'.

While young children must always be taught that jokes should never be used to *cause* distress, they do need to cope with the knowledge that some very bad things can happen – hence their eagerness for jokes about terrible things. Good videos for this type of survival humour include *The Simpsons* and most of Charlie Chaplin's films.

There is no shortage of films and television programmes that make people laugh: Buster Keaton, Laurel and Hardy, Danny Kaye's films, *The Simpsons*, *Garfield*, *Last of the Summer Wine*, *Whose Line Is It Anyway?*, *Open All Hours*, *Chef!*. Family programmes such as *The Cosby Show* can prove useful. For countering bullying, wholesome is better, because cynicism is linked to bitterness and depression.

To teach specific skills, such as ballet or cooking. Mastering a skill is an achievement which builds self-esteem. Building self-esteem is important in preventing bullying, and in rehabilitating both bullies and victims. People can enjoy even plain demonstrations on video of everything from handwriting and the alphabet to zoo-keepers' work. The advantage of being able to replay any section over and over without boring or exhausting the demonstrator is tremendous. Different styles or methods of performing an activity can be shown by excellent practition-ers. During   discussion, the appropriate section of tape can be played again if there is uncertainty or disagreement.

When pupils of any age see similar people doing things, they feel much more confident about their own potential to learn. If skills are used in an entertaining film they become attractive – the *MacGyver* television series inspired many girls and boys to study physics and/or chemistry for School Leaving Certificate. Dancers, gymnasts, pianists *et cetera* see muscles being used as they have been instructed to use theirs.

To counter bullying one must provide motivation and improve confidence and self-esteem. Videos teaching a skill can be of enormous help.

Finally, it is important to be aware that showing entertaining videos is a way of identifying bullies who need the services of a therapist for behaviour modification, and a counsellor to help them to sort out their thoughts and priorities. These are the bullies whose scorn and derision spoil everyone's pleasure. They need rehabilitation as a matter of urgency, for their own sake and for the protection of others. Children as young as seven can already be damaged in this way through copying older sibling's behaviour. This is no more pleasant for them than for those people, such as teachers, who are trying to cope with them.

Unfortunately, the symptoms are seldom recognised. When help is given, however, one of the methods used to rehabilitate these children and adolescents is the showing and discussion of entertaining videos.

Workplace Bullying

IS THERE such a thing as bullying in the workplace? What forms does it take? What effects does it have on individuals? Is it bad for business? Is there any relevant legislation? What good practices make bullying less likely? What can be done to reduce an intolerable level of bullying which is already well established?

The CaB definition of bullying is as follows: 'Bullying is abuse which causes only distress to the victim and gives gratification and power to the bully.' Another definition of workplace bullying is 'the abuse of power'. Bullying is gradually becoming the accepted general term for such abuse, covering areas such as violence, harassment and discrimination. It is prevalent wherever people work – hardly surprising given its prevalence in schools, neighbourhoods and family homes.

There is a common misconception that workplace bullying happens only among those employed in certain kinds of occupation. It is important to dispel that myth, as it reinforces the bullying and leads to defeatism among those who should be tackling it. For a crash course on forms and effects of workplace bullying, watch a couple of episodes of the excellent comedy series *Drop the Dead Donkey*.

The main forms of workplace bullying are:

- lack of consideration;
- bullying as part of 'tradition';
- grudge bullying;
- discrimination or harassment;
- overwork;
- stinginess;
- incompetence.

Lack of Consideration

This may be shown by bosses, management, workers, clients and customers. The bully may be motivated by rivalry or by any of a number of factors. It appears in various guises, often called 'poor communication'. Since information is power, one form of this abuse is the withholding of information from people who require it. The information withheld may be about entitlements and even about job specifications.

Another form of 'poor communication' is deliberate misinformation – the passing-on of information which is inaccurate and untrue, or which is partly true but misleading. The misinformation may include: taking credit for another's work and ideas; giving inaccurate information and bad advice as if being friendly and helpful; giving deliberately ambiguous instructions and then blaming the individual(s) for failure; character assassination; spreading true or false rumours that imply, unfairly, that someone is unfit for their work; rubbishing another's work by denying any merit in it and by exaggerating its flaws.

Misleading information and the withholding of information cause delays – one of the ways in which lack of consideration manifests itself as waste of someone's time. Time is valuable. Time is money. The bully's contention is: 'My time is valuable but yours is not.' The victim's time is being wasted by someone who is arrogant, incompetent or intent on causing inconvenience. If colleagues' response to a query is 'Find out', you must look everything up, keep your own files and reinvent the wheel, resulting in a time-consuming duplication of effort. Being forced to double-check everything is also time-consuming. When management gives instructions for which they do not have authority, most staff cope by saying, 'Once bitten, twice shy; I won't do what she wants again without checking that it's been cleared.' In the sense that it is inconsiderate and wastes time, misinformation is linked to poor attendance and poor punctuality – showing up late or not at all.

Sometimes this form of bullying is also a boycott, a kind of exclusion and isolation, where a group of people behave as if something or someone does not exist. Whether it's one colleague telling another, 'Don't attend his get-together' or 'Don't do business with that firm', or an authority figure banning a newspaper in the workplace or forbidding employees to send their children to a certain school, it is still bullying.

Bullying as Part of 'Tradition'

Initiation rites, other 'pranks', and office or works outings and parties can often be an occasion for bullying. Note the obvious connection with institutionalised school and social bullying which is also disguised as custom and fun, and which is perpetuated from one year to the next and condoned by all relevant authority figures. It is on record that initiation rites or pranks played to welcome the newcomer have sometimes resulted in the death of the unfortunate victim. New recruits should certainly be welcomed, but with courtesy and friendly behaviour, not with cruelty and mayhem. Tricks, pranks and practical jokes are an everyday plague for some, an occasional ordeal for others.

Bullying in the guise of traditional fun results in a pattern repeated over and over again – look at the similarity in the problems caused by silliness and drunkenness at celebrations for the school Junior Certificate results, the office Christmas party or summer outing, sports matches, engagement parties, stag nights, and Hallowe'en bonfire nights. Excessive consumption of alcohol is also part of the traditional image of certain occupations, and as such is often associated with felonies such as assaults, damage to property, intimidation, reckless driving, drug abuse, sexual assault, and ignoring statutory safety regulations and procedures.

Grudge Bullying

'On her way up the company she used to say that when she was in charge she was going to kick out the people she didn't like, and she named them. She's been in charge now for just three years. Now they've all gone – she made life impossible for them and they all left. Some are still very bitter, especially Mary, who is still out of work, and John, who took a constructive dismissal case against the company and won compensation.'

Employees with a grudge sometimes steal, ignore instructions, cause damage, or work slowly and sloppily.

People are most aware of bullying as discrimination or harassment. Some bullying managers go in for persistent picking on individuals, shouting at staff, making insulting personal remarks, calling staff members by offensive nicknames, public humiliation in any form, ignoring or cutting out an individual at meetings, addressing the individual only through third parties. They may also set someone up to fail by assigning them a task without giving necessary back-up or training. This, or scapegoating, will give them an excuse to remove areas of responsibility, but bullying managers may do this without any excuse and without warning, calling it reorganisation or restructuring. A victim of this form of bullying can find themselves in a non-job with nothing to do and nowhere to do it – office, telephone, everything gone.

A favourite ploy of the capricious office tyrant is to grant or refuse requests for leave (for funerals, weddings, dental appointments *et cetera*) purely on whim. Another is to insist that everything is treble-checked, effectively increasing the workload without increasing the amount of work produced.

Overwork

Overwork, whether caused by a boss's demands or by workaholism, is abuse. It may be the result of stinginess or incompetence. Sometimes the work to be done increases but no new staff are appointed; indeed it is not unusual to find staff numbers dropping as those who leave (for any reason) are not replaced. It is certainly an abuse of power if this happens in a company showing enormous profits, or in an area funded by a government department – such as Health or Education – from which the government have promised an improved service.

A stingy boss makes lack of money the excuse for ignoring safety regulations, and will cow employees by suggesting their jobs are on the line. Stingy employees can hold back a company's growth and damage its reputation by refusing to do anything not on their job specification, or by refusing to work for even one minute's overtime no matter how exceptional the circumstances.

Often workers complain about the distress they suffer because of the ignorance, incompetence and intransigence of their bosses; and the bosses abuse their power by refusing to listen, to learn or to change. Similarly, employees may abuse their power by ignoring directives and by not adopting new procedures taught to them on training courses on the grounds that 'They can't sack us all'.

The above gives a general picture of the forms bullying takes in the workplace. Denis Johnston called academe the most vicious of all worlds, even when compared to journalism and the law – a view supported by Sir Kenneth Dover's admission in his autobiography that he did not regret causing the death by suicide of a colleague by telling him his college wanted rid of him.

The Problems Caused by Workplace Bullying

According to the *Evening Press* of 1 December 1994, English employment lawyers Dibb Lupton Bloomhead are now advising corporate clients to sack all employees suffering from work-related stress because an unfair dismissals case will cost the firm less than a High Court ruling that it was to blame for the employee's nervous breakdown. This is very relevant information since bullying in the workplace causes enormous work-related stress.

The main symptoms of this stress are physical problems, including insomnia, headaches, allergies including eczema and asthma, irritable bowel syndrome, and reduced energy levels; plus psychological problems such as low motivation, depression, anxiety, anger, obsession with the bully which interferes with concentration so contributing to feeling slower, less competent, powerless, isolated and insecure. Stress lowers the immune response, making a sufferer more likely to succumb to viral and bacterial infections like flus, colds and tummy bugs. Where bullying causes overwork it can lead to burnout. Working to the point of exhaustion while ill with a viral infection can result in ME.

Bullying is bad for business, even if everybody is fairly happy and relaxed, because, as described above, it slows down communication and wastes time, and it results in the loss of millions of working-hours through accidents and injuries. Where there is stress there is further loss through stress-related illness and through the effect on staff morale, which tends to result in high rates of absenteeism.

Bullying stifles creativity and initiative. Where experienced staff leave or are forced out the loss to the firm can be very great. Productivity and the quality of the product are reduced by the effects of bullying, but profits also depend on factors other than the intrinsic value of what is produced. Bullying in the form of pollution, fraud and crime may seem financially successful, while in real terms the economy and the country suffer great loss.

Relevant Legislation

Assault, breach of the peace, larceny and intimidation are crimes. Under the Unfair Dismissals Act of 1977, a person can sue for unfair dismissal; a bullied employee can elect to leave the workplace and sue their former employer for constructive dismissal. The Employment Equality Act of 1977 deals with discrimination on the basis of sex and/or marital status. The Employment Equality Agency will give advice and information and will take cases where the case falls within their remit, which will be greatly extended under planned legislation from the Department of Equality and Law Reform. It is proposed to make unlawful at work sexual harassment (specifically) and general harassment on grounds of sexual orientation, age, disability, race, ethnic origin, including membership of the travelling community, colour and religion, parental or family status. Such harassment will be also unlawful in the context of the provision of goods and services. As well as the Safety in Industry Acts of 1955 and 1980, the Mines and Quarries Act 1965, the Dangerous

Substances Acts 1972 and 1979, and the European Communities Act 1972, there is the very important Safety, Health and Welfare at Work Act 1989 (and the Safety, Health and Welfare at Work (General Applications) Regulations 1993).

For information and advice, or to make a report, contact the Health and Safety Authority.

Every place of work must be covered by a safety statement. Note in particular that employees must take reasonable care for themselves and others, and must use any protective clothing and equipment which is provided. Under welfare arrangements, counselling must be available for all staff immediately after a violent incident; and staff must receive social and emotional support from immediate superiors and from management generally, as well as the use of any support services available for counselling. The term 'violence' as used here covers verbal abuse and threat of assault, as well as actual assault.

Workers' unions and employers' associations have codes of practice and guidelines on interpersonal relationships at work. There is, therefore, legislation on which to base good practices to make bullying less likely and to tackle bullying that is already prevalent.

Countering Bullying in the Workplace

A look at the forms bullying takes will suggest some obvious steps to take.

First, every worker needs a clear job specification, detailing in writing everything the job entails. Workers also need full information about rights and entitlements and the procedures for claiming these. They must be made aware of the safety statement, and of the employers' and employees' responsibilities in respect of safety.

Workers and employees need to know where to get information which they need at work: they need to know the right person to ask, whether they can consult files or documents; and, if so, how this information can be accessed. Once a worker has settled in, he will be more secure and more useful if he knows how the organisation works: who does what, who is in charge at each level or section. This information should be included in training instead of being picked up in a haphazard fashion.

Training should be clear and comprehensive with adequate supervision and back-up. In many firms some people receive training while others are thrown in at the deep end. As with peer-tutoring in schools, peer-training in businesses could help overloaded training officers ensure that no worker is floundering.

In order to establish and maintain good worker relationships, assertiveness training should be given to all personnel and subsequently to new intake shortly after arrival. This training goes a long way to preventing bullying and inconsiderate behaviour. Among other things, it will teach people how to avoid waste of their time.

Staff attach importance to knowing exactly what is expected of them, to being aware of the relative priorities of different aspects of their jobs, and to understanding where individual jobs fit into the priorities of the organisation. It is important that they receive continuous feedback on their performance, and support to achieve the highest possible levels of performance while developing their skills. The Performance Planning Review (PPR) process can be used to help the job-holder and her manager to plan and track the job-holder's performance in such a way that both the job-holder and the organisation's goals, including the development of skills and feedback on performance, are met.

Other important areas greatly helped by written forms and structures are compliments/complaints procedures and discipline/grievance procedures. Where these procedures are clearly laid out, the opportunity for bullying to arise or to continue unchecked is severely limited.

If management decides to reduce the level of bullying in their organisation, they must specify what matters may be cause for disciplinary action. Some forms of bullying, though not named as such, appear on many such lists, for example: violation of any criminal law; dishonesty; physical violence on duty; falsification, concealment or distortion of management information; wilful disobedience of reasonable orders; gross negligence; disorderly conduct on duty; verbal abuse on duty. It is important to stress that the main aim behind the disciplinary procedure is to provide a mechanism which signals that a problem exists, and which provides an employee with an opportunity to make good any shortfall in behaviour or performance. Once an allegation has been investigated, the employee may be exonerated. If the employee is at fault and the case is serious, dismissal or suspension may be appropriate. Repeated minor infringements attract increasingly serious sanctions, from a written warning through withdrawal of privileges, suspension of pay, probation, freezing of salary, reduction of salary, demotion to dismissal.

The legislation regarding welfare at work implies that management has a responsibility to take appropriate measures to prevent bullying in the workplace. Improving procedures for setting goals, and for complaints and discipline, would be a good start. In some occupations there need to be programmes aimed at changing established attitudes and traditional practices. Deglamorisation-of-alcohol programmes used in the US defence forces are an example of this sort of initiative already being implemented. Drama and role-play in prisons is another. Anything designed to increase an individual's humanity, sensitivity, empathy, sympathy and compassion, warmth, balance and sense of humour and appreciation of love and beauty is to be recommended. Many suggestions – from folk-dancing to games, from books to videos, from comfort to safety skills – are mentioned elsewhere in this book.

Fear is always a serious handicap in the fight against bullying. In the workplace fear of failure, of losing one's job, of losing business or customers, of losing a court case, of rivals or potential rivals, of competition or retribution, and of violence are strong. Only you can decide what is too risky for your taste. For anyone, a good place to start tackling bullying would be with the safety statement and the equality legislation.

FICTION USEFUL IN
COUNTERING BULLYING

Adams, Douglas: *The Hitchhiker's Guide to the Galaxy*, etc.

Alcott, L. M.: *Little Women, An Old-Fashioned Girl*, etc.

Andersen, H. C.: *The Ugly Duckling*, etc.

Austin, Jane: *Pride and Prejudice*, etc.

Belloc, Hilaire: *Children's Verses, Essays for Adults*, etc.

Callender, Don: *Pyromancer, Aquamancer*, etc.

Carroll, Lewis: *Alice in Wonderland* and *Through the Looking Glass*, etc.

Chant, Joy: *Red Moon and Black Mountain*.

Chesterton, G. K.: *The Napoleon of Notting Hill*; the Father Brown stories.

Cooper, Susan: *The Dark Is Rising* sequence.

Eddings, David: *The Belgariad*.

Emerson, Ru: *Night-threads* series, etc.

Heyer, G.: More than thirty delightful regency romances.

Hodgell, P. C.: *Chronicles of the Kencyrath*, etc.

Holt, Tom: *Expecting Someone Taller; Grailblazers*, etc.

Kipling, Rudyard: *The Jungle Book, Kim*, etc.

LeGuin, Ursula: *A Wizard of Earthsea*.

Lewis, C. S.: *The Lion, The Witch and the Wardrobe*, etc.

McKinley, Robin: *The Blue Sword*, etc.

Mackenzie, Compton: *Water on the Brain*, etc.

McKillip, Patricia: *Harper in the Wind*, etc.

Milne, A. A.: *Winnie the Pooh, The House at Pooh Corner*.

Montgomery, L. M.: *Emily Climbs, Anne of Ingleside*, etc.

Morressy, John: *Kedrigern in Wanderland*, etc.

Myers Myers, John: *Silverlock*.

Norton, Andre: *Witchworld*, etc.

Pratchett, Terry: *Discworld* series and all his other books too.

Sayers, Dorothy: *Lord Peter Wimsey* series.

Scott, Michael: *A Celtic Odyssey*, etc.

Shaw Gardner, Craig: *An Excess of Enchantments*, etc.

Thurber, James: '*The Secret Life of Walter Mitty*' etc.

Tolkien, J. R. R.: *The Hobbit, The Lord of the Rings*, etc.

Webster, Jean: *Daddy-Long-Legs, Dear Enemy*.

Willis, Connie: *Impossible Things*.

Wodehouse, P. G.: Everything, including the Jeeves and Wooster books.

Wynne-Jones, Diana: *Howl's Moving Castle; Archer's Goon,* etc.

Yates, Dornford: The *Berry* books, *The Stolen March*, etc.

PUBLICATIONS ON BULLYING

PLEASE note that in the Republic of Ireland, every school and public library has received from the Department of Education *Guidelines on Countering Bullying Behaviour in Primary and Post-Primary Schools* (1993). The Kidscape booklet *Stop Bullying* is available free from the ISPCC, 20 Molesworth Street, Dublin 2.

Every school in the UK has received, courtesy of the Calouste Gulbenkian Foundation, *Bullying: A Positive Response* by Delwyn Tattum and Graham Herbert; the information sheet 'Governors and Bullying', and *Bullying – The Child's View* by Jean La Fontaine. Also, the government has distributed to all UK schools *Action Against Bullying*, developed by SCRE, the Scottish Council for Research in Education. The Sheffield Research Pack is also available free to UK schools.

Most bookshops stock the following:
Bullying: A Practical Guide to Coping for Schools, edited by Michele Elliott (Longman).
Bullying at Work: How to Confront and Overcome It, Andrea Adams (Virago).
The Willow Street Kids, Michele Elliott (Piccolo/Andre Deutsch).

Particularly useful for researchers are:
Bullying: An Annotated Bibliography of Literature and Resources, Alison Skinner, available from the National Youth Agency, 17-23 Albion Street, Leicester LE1 6GD.
Bullies and Victims in Schools, Valerie Besag (Open University Press).
Bullying at School: What We Know and What We Can Do, Dan Olweus (Blackwell Press).
Bullying in Schools (1988), Mona O'Moore, Council of Europe report DECS-EGT(88)5-E (Strasbourg Council for Cultural Cooperation).

'Bullying in Dublin Schools', AM O'Moore and B Hillery (*Irish Journal of Psychology* 10, 3, 426-441)

'Bullying in School', Mona O'Moore (*Curam* 17, NPC – Primary).

Proceedings of the First National Conference on Bullying in Ireland (1993). Published by CaB in September 1994 and available from CaB, 72 Lakelands Avenue, Stillorgan, Co. Dublin – tel. (01) 288 7976.

RESOURCES AND CONTACT POINTS

Republic of Ireland

The Sticks and Stones Theatre Company (01) 280 7065.
This company premiered its play for primary schools at the CaB conference in March 1993, its play for parents' groups at the NAPS seminar in October 1994, and its play for secondary schools at Kings Hospital in January 1995. Its outstandingly successful primary-school programme includes a visit by the facilitator, a teacher's handbook, the performance, and classroom discussions.

The National Association for Parents Support Capoley, Portlaoise, Co. Laois (0502) 20598.
NAPS provides leaflets and newsletters, holds seminars and a drop-in centre. It may be contacted on all matters connected with education, and also for information, advice and support for bullying problems.

Barnardo's National Children's Resource Centre, Christchurch Square, Dublin 8 (01) 453 0355.
Also hosts the Children's Rights Alliance.

The Campaign Against Bullying, 72 Lakelands Avenue, Stillorgan, Co. Dublin.

Education Matters, 47 Watson Avenue, Killiney, Co. Dublin (01) 285 1696.
A magazine and radio programme for parents, students and teachers and all those interested in education.

The Irish Red Cross Society, 16 Merrion Square, Dublin 2 (01) 676 5135.
Many services, ranging from training in safety skills to entertainment by clowns.

Youthworks, The National Youth Federation, 20 Lower Dominick Street, Dublin 7 (01) 872 9933.
Library, seminars, reports et cetera.

Irish Youth Foundation, 1 Ringsend Road, Dublin 4 (01) 660 2933.

National Youth Council, 3 Montague Street, Dublin 2 (01) 478 4122.

Unicef, 4 St Andrew's Street, Dublin 2 (01) 677 0843.

CAPP: The Child Abuse Prevention Programme, Stay Safe Unit, The Lodge, Cherry Orchard Hospital, Ballyfermot, Dublin 10 (01) 623 2358.

Parents Alone Resource Centre, Bunratty Drive, Coolock, Dublin 17 (01) 848 1872.
Produced resource book *Mothers and Breadwinners*.

Health and Safety Authority, 10 Hogan Place, Dublin 2 (01) 662 0400.

Employment Equality Agency, 36 Upper Mount Street, Dublin 2 (01) 660 5966.

Department of Education (01) 873 4700. Press office (01) 874 2372.

Self Defence for Women and Children (01) 289 2044/283 2401.

Northern Ireland

Education and Library Board, 40 Academy Street, Belfast, BT12 NQ; Campsi House, Hospital Road, Omagh, Co Tyrone, BT79 0AW; Graham's Bridge Road, Dundonald, Belfast, BT1 60HS.

Scotland

The Scottish Council for Research in Education, 15 St John's Street, Edinburgh EH8 8JR.

Strathclyde Region Education Department, Clyde House, 170 Kilbourne Road, Clydebank, Glasgow G81.
Scottish Consultative Council on the Curriculum

Information and Marketing Services, Gardyne Road, Broughty Ferry, Dundee DD5 1NY.

Moray House Institute of Education, Heriot-Watt University, Cramond Road North, Edinburgh Eh4 6JD.

ACAS Advisory Service (041) 204 2677.

England

Advisory Centre for Education – also covers Wales (0171) 354 8321.

Bullying

Anti-Bullying Campaign (0171) 378 1446.

Kidscape, 152 Buckingham Palace Road, London SW1 9TR (0171) 730 3300.

Professor PK Smith, Department of Psychology, PO Box 603, University of Sheffield, S10 2UR.

Val Besag, 57 Manor House Road, Jesmond, Newcastle upon Tyne, NE2 2LY.

Professor Peter Randall and Mike Donoghue, Department of Social Policy and Professional Studies, University of Hull also The North Hull Community Anti-Bullying Project (0482) 858585.

National Youth Agency (0533) 471 200.

ACAS Advisory Service (0171) 210 3000.

Wales

Delwyn Tattum, South Glamorgan Institute of Higher Education, Cyncoed Road, Cardiff CF2 6XD (0222) 551111.

ACAS Advisory Service (0222) 762636.

All of these have contacts with other countries – for example, Hull with Holland and Germany. Note that Hull's project deals with bullying in the home, the neighbourhood, the workplace and all institutions, including schools.

Switzerland

Christopher Szaday, ZBS, Zentralschweizerischer, Beratungschenst fur Schulfragen, Luzernerstrasse 69, 6030 Ebikon (041) 36 59 13.

Australia

Institute of Social Research, University of South Australia, North Terrace, Adelaide, S Australia 5000 (08) 302 2403/2183.

Australian Council for Educational Research, Radford house, 9 Frederick Street, Hawthorn, Victoria 3122 .

Coosje Griffiths, Darling Range District Education Office, 36 Railway Parade, Midland, Western Australia 6056 (09) 453 6666/384 4598.

Index

accountability *see* blame

achievement *5-9, 55, 60, 125, 154,
156*; high achievers *7*, as bullies *7*,
as victims *7*; low achievers *5, 6*, as
bullies *8-9*, as victims *8-9*, as
bully-victims *25*, unmotivated *9*;
middling achievers *7-8*, as bullies
7, as victims *8*

acronyms *10-11*

action *12-14, 22, 153*; considering a
course of *14*; in rehabilitating
bully-victims *126*

adult bullies *121*

Alcoholics Anonymous *121*

anger *124*

Anne of Windy Willows 13

Archers Goon (TV series) *155*

arts, appreciation of *153*

assertiveness training *58-9*

attention seeking *127*

attitudes to bullying: need to change
57, 62, 67

authority *5, 12, 15-17, 86, 95, 127,
134*; authority figures attacked by
bullies *15*

avoiding bullying *18-22*

backronyms *10*

Beauty and the Beast (film) *152, 155*

blame *23-4*

bristle factor *65*

bullies *10, 49-50, 57, 59, 67*;
challenging *135. See also* bullying,
rehabilitation bullying: definitions
of *36, 48-9, 80, 158*; theories of
133; myths about *16, 132, 134*; in
classroom *7-9*, excuses for *84-95*

bully-victims *10, 25-6, 50, 120, 123*;
rehabiliation of *125-30, 147*

bystanders *27-30*; responses to
bullying *28-30*

Bullying at Work (Adams) *123*

Campaign against Bullying *31-9, 131*

catchphrases *152*

challenging bullies *27*

Chef! (TV series) *152*

class charter *45, 47*

classroom atmosphere *47*

classroom management *40-7, 60-1*

Cleary, Father Michael *142*

clubs *35, 125*

code of conduct *see* school rules

competition *22, 51*

communication *13*

confidence *6, 43, 54, 156*

confrontation *1*

contracts *49, 122, 128-9*

control *74*

cooperation *22, 42, 129*

Cosby Show, The (TV series) *156*

counselling *50*

course against bullying *48-53*

course of action *see* action

customs *53*

Dad's Army (TV series) *152*

dance *49, 50, 51, 52, 54-6*

Dangerous Substances Acts 1972,
1979 *163-4*

deceit *see* lies

denial *84, 89-90*

diet *124*

disability *8*; bullying of those with
57-61; effects on family *61;*
discipline *47, 49, 87*; in workplace
165-6

Discipline in the Primary School
(INTO) *112*

discrimination, workplace *158*;
see also prejudice, racism

diversity, valuing *64*

doubt, cast on victims *91-2*

Dover, Sir Kenneth *152*

Drop the Dead Donkey (TV series)
158

dyslexia *128*

effective retaliation *22*

empathy *58, 61, 65*

Employment Equality Act 1977 *163*

Employment Equality Agency *163*

OTHER RELEVANT BOOKS

From Attic Press

Hooked?
Young People Drugs & Alcohol
by Yvonne Ward
£7.99 ISBN 1 85594 082 5
Hooked? deals with all kinds
of addiction and substance abuse,
amongst young people from
solvents to alcohol, soft
drugs and hard drugs. Hooked?
introduces the reader to some
young addicts and lets them
tell their own story.
Yvonne Ward, psychologist
is also the author of
A Bottle In The Cupboard
Women & Alcohol

Your Breaking Point:
Effective Steps to Reduce
and Cope with Stress
by Dolores Whelan
£7.99 ISBN 1 85594 071 X
The book looks at the typical
symptoms of stress, outlines
the common personality types,
compiles stress profiles and
clearly details simple ways to
find relief.